Once Upon a Rhyme

Poets From The Midlands

Edited by Helen Davies
& Donna Samworth

First published in Great Britain in 2011 by:

Young Writers

Young Writers
Remus House
Coltsfoot Drive
Peterborough
PE2 9BF
Telephone: 01733 890066
Website: www.youngwriters.co.uk

All Rights Reserved
Book Design by Tim Christian
© Copyright Contributors 2010
SB ISBN 978-0-85739-336-4

THIS BOOK BELONGS TO

....

Foreword

Here at Young Writers our objective is to help children discover the joys of poetry and creative writing. Few things are more encouraging for the aspiring writer than seeing their own work in print. We are proud that our anthologies are able to give young authors this unique sense of confidence and pride in their abilities.

Once Upon A Rhyme is our latest fantastic competition, specifically designed to encourage the writing skills of primary school children through the medium of poetry. From the high quality of entries received, it is clear that Once Upon A Rhyme really captured the imagination of all involved.

The resulting collection is an excellent showcase for the poetic talents of the younger generation and we are sure you will be charmed and inspired by it, both now and in the future.

Contents

Maddie Stewart is our featured poet this year. She has written a nonsense workshop for you and included some of her great poems. You can find these in the middle of your book.

Sandy Innocent (9) 1

Badsey First School, Badsey
Robyn Dare (9) 1
Lucy Trevorrow (9) 2
Morgan Bartlett (10) 2
Claudia Agrusa (9) 3
Ryan Keyte (9) 3
Lexie Evans (9) 4
John Barradell (9) 4
Kaylee Thompson (9) 5
Cameron Warmington (9) 5
George Kirby (9) 6
Kieran Spiers (9) 6
Holly-Anne Chinn (9) 7
Joe Cook (9) 7
Shauna Parker (9) 7
Ryan Smith (9) 8
Libby Foster (8) 8
Libby Salter (9) 8
Frances Seabrook (8) 9
Bradley Cornfield (9) 9
Ben Holland (9) 9
Emily-Paris Hirst (9) 10
Chloe Holland (8) 10
Charlotte Howlett (8) 10
James Goode (10) 11
Isabelle Middleton (8) 11
Hannah Beckley (9) 11
Stephen Bridges (9) 12
Sam Dean (9) 12
Adam Ballard (9) 12
Molly Morris (8) 12
Immy Smith (8) 13
Rebecca Phillips (8) 13
Oliver Hampton (8) 13

Brockhampton Primary School, Worcester
Joe Green (9) 13
Brooke Stancliffe (9) 14
Laura Wilks (9) 14
Tom Baker (9) 14
Angus Gibbs (9) 15
Tom Hutchinson (11) 15

Burlish Park Primary School, Stourport-on-Severn
Morgan Yarrington-Bull (9) 15
Thomas Allen (10) 16
Daniel Stokes (9) 17
Sarah Daniels (10) 18
Matthew Adams (10) 18
Grace Baldwin (9) 19
Mark Westcott (10) 19
Phoebe Francis (10) 20
Sophie Condon (10) 20
Liam Shelton (10) 21
Safronne Lee (9) 21
Jordan Rigby (10) 22
Kieran Russell (10) 22
Emily Jones (10) 23

Jasmine Canty (10)	23
Alex Rose (10)	24
Bradley Worton (10)	24
Izzy Prescott (10)	25
Meghan Turner (11)	25
Amy Breakwell (11)	26
Kieran O'Neill (9)	26
Megan Oliver (11)	27
Shannon Bradley (9)	27
Lucy Rollins (10)	28
Ellie Blaze (10)	28
Daniel Roby (9)	29
Jessica McPhee (9)	29
Callum Parry (9)	30
Stephanie Whaile (10)	30
Louisa Garland (9)	31
Amy Lewis (11)	31
Olivia Turner (9)	32
Emily Rose Carrier (10)	32
Dylan Moreton (10)	33
Charlotte Voysey (10)	33
Joe Waldron (10)	34
Seona Davies (10)	34
Ben Napthine (11)	35
Emma Parsons (11)	35
Harry Deacon (10)	36
Megan Lloyd (10)	36
Ryan Harper (10)	37
Danielle O'Neill (10)	37
Ben Evans (9)	38
Ellis Troth (11)	38
Bradley Mason (10)	39
Alex Jones (9)	39
Nathan David Farmer (9)	40
Jessica Barrett (10)	40
Georgia Little (10)	41
Chloe Davies (9)	41
Jordan Rowbottom (10)	42
Sam Turbutt (10)	42
Dan Rowley (10)	42
Daniel Bell (9)	43
Lucy Elliott (11)	43
Lucy McLatchy (9)	43
Elsie Cole (9)	44
Ben Voyce (10)	44
Becky Edwards (9)	44
Ryan Cadwallader (10)	45
Megan Bush (9)	45

Feckenham CE First School, Redditch

Anna Nicod (8)	45
Alex Oldcorn (8)	46
Luke Tait (8)	46
Megan Griffiths (8)	47
Mia Crowe (8)	47
Lucy Gibbs (8)	48
Katie Willis-Ball (8)	48
Alexander Guilfoyle (9)	48
Luke Wade (9)	49
Harry Read (8)	49
Olivia Grace Pearce (8)	49
Rhian Tye (8)	49

Holmer Lake Primary School, Telford

Fred Foley (7)	50
Keavy Evans (10)	50
Caitlin Morgan (8)	51
Brandon Rowson-Streames	51
Robert Gibbons (10)	52
Matthew Kershaw (9)	52
Karl Kellam (7)	53
Tiffany Owen (9)	53
Jeremy Abbey (7)	54
Daniel Gunnell (10)	54
Lewis Surgenor (10)	55
Francesca Blair-Haines (9)	55
Katelyn Fletcher (7)	56
Dylan Gillett (10)	56
Ethan Lamb (7)	57
Jack Williams (11)	57
Alex Clayton (10)	58
Joshua Thomas (10)	58
Courtney Dean (7)	59
Lauryn Proudman (10)	59
Kai Mason (8)	60
Anika Francis (7)	60
Bonnie Boylett (7)	61
Isha Mal (8)	61
Abigail Hopley (10)	62
Corey Thomas (8)	62

Katie Edwards (10) 63
Owen Kershaw (8) 63
Sean Clancy (9) 64
Ellie Kearney (8) 64
Meagan Jones (8) 65
Ebonie Thomas (10) 65
Natasha Laine (9) 65
Jamie Barnes (11) 66
Kirsty Webster (10) 66

Little Dewchurch CE Primary School, Hereford
Libby Bailey (7) 66
Zack Jenkins (10) 67
Laura Simpkins (7) 67
Marcus Bailey (9) 68
Jayden Dare (9) 68
Amie Jenkins (8) 69
Edward Charles (10) 69
Esme Lang (7) 70
Benjamin Tate (8) 70
Bethany Aldsworth (10) 71
Melissa Louise Peters (8) 71
Lauren Legge (8) 72
Nick Peters (10) 72
Susan Hawker (8) 73
Ellis Shepherd (7) 73

Loatlands Primary School, Kettering
Calista Turnell (11) 73
Rebecca Lindy Ainsworth 74
Hattie Rose Street (10) 74

Marlbrook Primary School, Hereford
Jaime Anderson (9) 74
Daisy Morris (9) 75
Benjamin Nelder (9) 75
Alexis Foster (9) 76
Loren Prothero (9) 76
Jasmine Edkins (10) 89
James Venables (10) 89
Mia Rumsey (9) 90
Tyler Chatterley-Russell (10) 90
Spencer Young (7) 90
Lauren Perkins (9) 91
Curtis Jenkins (11) 91
Rachelle Jaine Barrall (10) 91

Alexander Baker (9) 92
Callum Harding (9) 92
Marshall Turner (9) 92
Lucy Silver (7) 93
Keaton Glancy (10) 93
Dominica Allfrey (10) 93
Candice Hooper (7) 94
Ashleigh Jenkins (9) 94
Lauren Francis (9) 94
Chloe Grant (9) 95
Dylan Jones (9) 95
Chloe Pegrum (9) 95
Bethany Mason (7) 96
Imogen Lavell (9) 96
Abbie Crawford (10) 96
Caitlin Bethell (10) 96
James Oakley (10) 97
Saffron Scott (8) 97
Emilie May Preedy (7) 97

Norbury Primary School, Bishops Castle
Charlotte Hughes (8) 97
Braden Colley (8) 98
Charlotte Muller (10) 98
Anni Lloyd-Langford (7) 99
Jake Varcoe (10) 99
Grace Davies (7) 100
Rohan Colley (8) 100
Jodie Betton (10) 100
Kirsty Betton (8) 101
Amelia Jones (10) 101
Sophie Gillin (10) 101
Rebecca Speich (7) 102
Louis Wood (10) 102
Millie Wood (8) 102
Olivia Littlehales (8) 103
Milo Turner (7) 103
Lola McCormack (9) 103
Sally Watney (7) 103
Tom Jarratt (7) 104

Perrywood Primary & Nursery School, Worcester
Annabel Holt (10) 104
Sian Hammett (10) 104

Travis Wiggins (10)	105
Niamh Hammett (10)	105
Lewis Mitchell Hartley (10)	105
Todd Edgington (10)	106
Joshua Heywood (10)	106
Laurence Canoy (10)	106

St Andrew's CE Primary School, Stafford

Tom Daykin (10)	107
Finley Joseph Morris (10)	108
Gisela Ashley (10)	109
Jacob Ratcliffe (10)	110
Megan Washburn (10)	111
Natasha Yewdell (10)	112
Zoe Wright (11)	113
Sophie Thomas (10)	114
Callum Coates (11)	115
Isabelle Clews (10)	115
Lucy Greenall (10)	116

St Margaret's CE Junior School, Whitnash

Nikita Kohli (10)	116
Taiya Cooper (7)	117

St Thomas More Catholic School, Kettering

Clara Soto (9)	117
Erin Walsh (9)	118
Lucy Bishop (10)	119
Jordan Elliot (9)	119
Alice Ball (10)	120
Leah Meghen (9)	121
Joe Massaro (9)	121
Aodán Farrell (9)	122
Myles Fletcher (9)	122
Edward Tolentino (9)	123
Anna Tew (9)	123
Matthew Druery (9)	124
Rieno Tartaglia (9)	124
Leilia White (9)	125
James Wiles (9)	125
Luke Pallett (9)	125
George Sansone (9)	126
Daniel Hakobyan Pereira (9)	126
Nicole Pedro (9)	126

Emilia Berardi-Ross (9)	127
Isabella Novaga (9)	127
Eva Grace Pointer (9)	127
Carys Smith (10)	128
Brooke Willis (9)	128
Harrison Fawcett (10)	128
Courtney Rusike (9)	129
Charley Burke (10)	129

Simon De Senlis Primary School, Northampton

J R (10)	129
Amy Bean (9)	130
Ellie Thorpe (9)	131
Callum Perrin (10)	131
Ayo Arowolo (9)	132
Jamie Hayday (9)	132
Matthew Duffy (10)	133
Sam Nurse (10)	133
Kate Skinner (9)	134
Chloe Higgins-White (9)	134
Evie Stanton (9)	135
Tia Binks (10)	135
Jasmin Cox (10)	136
Lewis Bradley (9)	136
Ash Tailor (8)	137
Jade Walter (10)	137
Jordan Harrison (9)	138
Kelson Gibbons (10)	138
Tia Binks (10)	139
David Obreja (10)	139
Oliver Fosbury (9)	140
Len Mwaura (9)	140
Abbie Reboul (9)	141
Gabriella Teriaca (10)	141
Ryan Wright (10)	142
William Jack Rainbow	142
Rhumer Kay (11)	143
Megan Schofield (9)	143
Shivani Sehmi	144
Emily Nicklin (10)	144
Bhavika Mistry (9)	144
Jasmin West (10)	145
Natasha Partridge (10)	145
Jamie Vaughan (9)	145
Nathan Cox (10)	146

Olivia Dugmore (10) ... 146
Callum Kennedy (9) ... 146
Jamie Collingwood (10) ... 147
Hannah Chisholm (10) ... 147
Chloe Scott (10) ... 147
Poppy Jones (10) ... 148
Ella Clarke (10) ... 148
Lewis Gilmour (11) ... 148
Christopher Amankonah (10) ... 149
Joshua Nkire (10) ... 149
Rajinder Singh Thandi (10) ... 149
Tyler Paul Allen Maishment (10) ... 150
Olivia Wingrove (11) ... 150
Jack Baker (10) ... 150
Husna Khawaja (10) ... 151
Chloe Holder (10) ... 151
Keanu Cross (10) ... 151
Bradley Luis-Hobbs (10) ... 152
Jordan Glentworth (10) ... 152
Jack Dredge (10) ... 152
Jack Smith (10) ... 152
Lucy Marsh (10) ... 153
Elizabeth Powell (11) ... 153
Edward Barrett (10) ... 153
Ciara Mulcahy (10) ... 153
CJ Mlilo (11) ... 154
Bethany Lam (9) ... 154
Megan Topham (9) ... 154
Bethany Winter (10) ... 154
Rhys Jenkins (10) ... 155

Stanwick School, Stanwick
Lucy Irons (9) & Faith Burrill (10) ... 155
Charlotte Irons (9) ... 155
Isabelle Aubrey (9) ... 156
Natasha Blakemore (9) ... 156
Nathaniel Gyngell (9) ... 156
Emma Brown (10) ... 157
Zach Martin-Sinclair (10) ... 157
Amy Delauney (9) ... 157
Elise Hodge (9) ... 158
Joshua Dawson (9) ... 158
Rory Vartanian (9) ... 158

Whitchurch CE Junior School, Whitchurch
Brodie Edge (7) ... 158
Charles Smith (7) ... 159
Megan Stokes (7) ... 159
Tiffany Chan (7) ... 160
Abby Rooney (7) ... 160
Cameron Jones (7) ... 161
Tilly Evanson (7) ... 161
Holly Millerchip (7) ... 161
James Maddocks (7) ... 162
Owen Kinsey (7) ... 162
Tyler Ashley (7) ... 163
Alex Williams (8) ... 163

The Poems

If I Had £1,000 Pounds

If I had £1,000 I'd buy a pure gold teddy,
If I had £1,000 I'd call my teddy Freddy.
If I had £1,000 I'd buy a big TV,
If I had £1,000 I'd have a big party.
If I had £1,000 I'd buy a jumbo jet,
If I had £1,000 I'd have no homework set.
If I had £1,000 I'd make a glow-in-the-dark hairspray,
If I had £1,000 I'd have a place to play.

Sandy Innocent (9)

Sockey Man

Sockey Man is great,
Sockey Man is cool,
Sockey Man's so brilliant,
He makes you want to drool.

He is a superhero,
He flies around the world,
He rescues damsels in distress,
That have their hair curled.

Sockey Man is a sock
And his stripes are pink and green,
Sockey Man can fly so fast,
That he's barely ever seen.

Sockey Man is strong,
Very strong indeed,
He is so strong he makes
Batman look like a weed.

Sockey Man has a great time,
Though he thinks it would be nice,
Just to chill out for a while
And have a cold drink with ice!

Robyn Dare (9)
Badsey First School, Badsey

Chickens Galore

I have three chickens, well, I used to.
Their names were: Star, Bluebell and Speckledy,
Bluebell was my favourite even though she died first,
Because she didn't eat anything!

I have five chickens, well I used to,
Their names were: Oven-Ready and Drumstick,
Chocolate and Cocoa too,
But you must not forget Brownie,
She didn't mind being picked up,
Plus she was so cute!
But the problem is . . . she . . . didn't respond.

Here is an example:
You go, '*Chook, chook, chook*!'
Nothing.
You try again.
Still nothing.

I now have no chickens,
Mum and Dad said,
'We might get some more after Christmas,'
Though . . . I think . . .

Lucy Trevorrow (9)
Badsey First School, Badsey

Me And My Dad

My dad is six foot two,
Normally he can't fit through the door!
Sometimes I think he's a deadly tickler,
Because he tickled my brother and wouldn't stop.
Now he's sixteen he doesn't do it anymore.
When I go to bed, that's half-nine,
He hides behind the door and says, 'Boo!'
I always end up falling over,
Then I say, 'Don't you do that!'
He starts to laugh.
I'm like *grr* then I go into the kitchen,
I get a drink of orange,
Then I go to bed.

Morgan Bartlett (10)
Badsey First School, Badsey

My Family

Hi, let me introduce you to my family,
First there's my mum, Tina, she is really nice.
She works at my school as a lunchtime supervisor.
Next we have my dad, Giovanni, he is Italian and he lives in Lichfield,
Where he works in his friend's restaurant as a waiter.
Then we have my sister, Gabbie,
She goes to Prince Henry's High School,
She loves loud music
And chatting to her friends on her mobile phone
And the computer.
Now we have my nan, Joan,
She often says to me, 'Do you want a biscuit?'
I sometimes say, 'Yes please, Nan.'
My nan often goes to bingo at the British Legion.
She also loves the telly.
Finally we have me, Claudia,
I love animals and making cakes with my mum.
I sometimes say to my mum,
'Mum, are the cakes ready yet?'
She says, 'No not yet, just give them another five minutes.'

Claudia Agrusa (9)
Badsey First School, Badsey

My Gerbil

He may look cute
He may look cuddly,
But my old gerbil's
Deadly
I took him to the
Pictures and sat
Him on my knee
All he did was nibble me.
He's deadly!
I put him in his cage
Then I went to bed
I woke up in the morning
And found him dead.
My old gerbil really is deadly!

Ryan Keyte (9)
Badsey First School, Badsey

Sleepovers

I love it when my friends come for a sleepover,
We play games and do weird dances,
Then we go to bed,
That's when the fun starts,
My parents say, 'Goodnight,' and, 'Go to sleep now!'
But we don't,
When they get out we eat, talk, even play music,
Then we hear the creak of the floorboards outside my room,
We know we've only got seconds,
It's all silent; sweets stuffed under pillows, mouths shut,
We lie there silent,
It's not till we see through the corner of our eyes
The light fades as the door closes and we know it's safe to breathe again!
Phew, *chomp, chomp*, la, la, la!

Lexie Evans (9)
Badsey First School, Badsey

What Are Dads?

What are dads? Are they grubby little things
That live under the fridge or maybe they're
Fat horrible giants?
They must be in disguise.
What's the point of them?
Who knows, well at least my nose doesn't.
On Monday they moan and groan,
Tuesday,
They eat a lot of chocolate, on Wednesday they
Worry if you watch too much Wolverine and the X-Men,
And on Friday they get a ferry to France,
And I'm not even
Going to talk about the weekend,
I wonder what they really are.

John Barradell (9)
Badsey First School, Badsey

My Brother

Brothers are nice one minute,
Horrible the next,
They sit in the seat,
You're just going to sit in.
They nick your sweets, peanuts and crisps,
Cheese and onion, his favourite,
I say, 'Do you want one?'
He doesn't take one, he takes three million.
So I played a little trick on him,
I put seven apples under his mattress.
That night he got into bed and said,
'What is that?'
I said, 'Look under your mattress.'
He said, 'Kaylee.'

Kaylee Thompson (9)
Badsey First School, Badsey

The Book

I was watching TV when *kaboom!*
A scream from my brother,
A mysterious object was on the table,
'What's that?' I said.
'It's a book,' replied Mum
'A-a-a b-book. Are you trying to kill us?
We need TV not that!'

'I'll have a go,' I said
It got tense in the room
I opened it . . .
'Argh!' I slammed it shut.
'It's maths,' I said to my brother.
We both fainted.

Cameron Warmington (9)
Badsey First School, Badsey

A Ball

They invented a new ball,
A new bouncy ball,
A new bouncy, red ball.

I so wanted the new ball,
I really wanted the new bouncy ball,
I really, really wanted the new bouncy, red ball.

I waited for my birthday to get the new ball,
I waited for weeks for my birthday to get the new bouncy ball.
I waited for months for my birthday to get the new bouncy, red ball.

It's my birthday, have I got the new bouncy, red ball?
'Yes I have got the new bouncy, red ball,
Yipee! Yipee!' I can now play with my new bouncy, red ball.

George Kirby (9)
Badsey First School, Badsey

My Bike

My bike is black.
I like riding it.
It has 2 stunt pegs
And I can do big wheelies on it.

When I do big wheelies sometimes
I tip to the side and fall off!

'Why is that?'

Maybe I lean to the side slightly
Without realising.
Maybe I go down a pothole.
Maybe my ears are lopsided!

Kieran Spiers (9)
Badsey First School, Badsey

My Dad And My Snake

Dad asks a lot of questions about my snake
I've got used to it now,
He'd say, 'Why has your snake got a lump in the middle of him?'
I'd say, 'He has just had his dinner and his name is Coby not Snake.'
A few days later he'd say, 'Why's that snake of yours extremely wet?'
I'd say, 'He has just had a bath in his water dish and his name is Coby not Snake!'
In the morning Dad shouts,
'The snake has gone!'
'His name is Coby not Snake!'
At the end of the day he's say, 'What's his name again?'
'Uh, I give up!'

Holly-Anne Chinn (9)
Badsey First School, Badsey

WRVS

Working together, that's what we do
Delivering meals to people just like you
That's how we make it count
Make it count more or less
Down in the kitchen at the WRVS.

Now we deliver to the rich and we deliver to the poor
We deliver frozen meals right up to your door
That's how we make it count
Make it count more or less
Down in the kitchen at the WRVS
Yes down in the kitchen at the WRVS.

Joe Cook (9)
Badsey First School, Badsey

Cats' Tails

Cats have tails,
They like to go to Wales,
They love sails,
They like to eat snails,
They're scared of whales.

Shauna Parker (9)
Badsey First School, Badsey

Me And My Brother

My brother, Ben, was born on October the second
And I was happy when my brother, Ben, was born
Then I went back to my gran's house late.
I went to sleep
The next day my brother, Ben, picked me up from my gran's
With my mum and dad
When they came in the house, I felt happy,
Then I went back to my house with Ben and my mum and dad,
When we got in my house I played with Ben,
Later I played on the Xbox for an hour,
Then I went to sleep.

Ryan Smith (9)
Badsey First School, Badsey

Ponies And Horses

Ponies trot
Horses gallop
All around you
Across fields
And plains
They like
To canter
And ponies
Like to be
Ridden all
Around you.

Libby Foster (8)
Badsey First School, Badsey

My Mum

Me and Mum went to the park to play,
I went to the shop to buy some sweets and a CD,
We spent £10,
When we got home I helped my mum to cook the tea,
It was very yummy
When it was dark we went to bed.

Libby Salter (9)
Badsey First School, Badsey

Autumn

In autumn the leaves begin to fall,
Twisting and twirling as they go,
From the trees so tall,
Colours bright and some dull
Yellow, brown and red.

As you kick the autumn leaves,
Up they jump like fireflies,
Dancing as they catch the wind,
Then lying still on the ground.

Frances Seabrook (8)
Badsey First School, Badsey

Me And Tom

Going from day to day I like to play.
My brother, Tom, always plays football with me.
I really enjoy playing football with him because he teaches me tricks and also makes me laugh, 'Watch me do this bicycle kick, Brad!'
The he falls over!
When I play for my football team,
He always tries to come and watch.
My brother, Tom, also comes to tae kwon do with me
And we both enjoy it together.

Bradley Cornfield (9)
Badsey First School, Badsey

Me And My Dog

Me and my dog go out for walks,
We take a ball with us.
She loves chasing after balls in fields with nice short grass.
She likes to go paddling in the rivers, swimming like a duck.
We throw sticks for her and she brings them back,
She loves the snow and the sun.
Sometimes we say, 'Where has she gone? Has she gone down the field chasing a rabbit?'
We all laugh!

Ben Holland (9)
Badsey First School, Badsey

My Dog's Poem

When my dog was a puppy
We had thought of lots of names.
My dad saw a Hugo Boss bag and said,
'What about Hugo?'
We all said yes and that was settled.
Next we chose him and he was the one.
He's very bouncy and everyone loves him.
He is so soft.
I love him.

Emily-Paris Hirst (9)
Badsey First School, Badsey

Butterfly

Butterfly, butterfly,
Fly away,
Butterfly, butterfly,
Land again,
Butterfly, butterfly,
Fly so tall,
Butterfly, butterfly,
Please don't fall.

Chloe Holland (8)
Badsey First School, Badsey

Maths

When my teacher says to add
It makes me feel really sad.
But when it's time to take away
I want to shout *'Hip hip hooray.'*
Then as we start to multiply
I get a twinkle in my eye.
And as we divide (or share)
I'm so happy - I haven't a care!

Charlotte Howlett (8)
Badsey First School, Badsey

ONCE UPON a RHYME -- Poets From The Midlands

Gertie

Gertie's there when I go to my gran's house,
Gertie is always there.
She's so mad and jumps up and starts scratching your legs
And keeps on doing it.
She is really fun to play with; every time she's good I give her a treat.
She likes to lick your hand, when you put your hand low she licks it.
Sometimes me, Adam and my grandad go for a walk with her to the park.
When we go she gets sad and is lonely.

James Goode (10)
Badsey First School, Badsey

Maisy

We have a dog called Maisy
She's extremely lazy
She has a hairy chin
Which is always wet
And when she's ill we take her to the vet
She wags her tail when she's happy
And she's never ever snappy.

Isabelle Middleton (8)
Badsey First School, Badsey

My Bird Spot

I have a bird called Spot
He likes nibbling people's fingers!
His favourite food is cucumber
He sits in his gold cage saying,
'What you doing? What you doing?'
When he comes out he flies all around the room
And before you know it he's on my head!

Hannah Beckley (9)
Badsey First School, Badsey

Run Patch

'Run Patch! Run Patch!' That's my dog.
'Run Patch! Run Patch!' Through the wind.
'Run Patch! Run Patch! Fetch that stick.
'Run Patch! Run Patch! Don't look back.
'Run Patch! Run Patch! Aren't you out of breath yet?'
After I stroke Patch I say, 'What a very fantastic dog you are!'
He just replies, *woof, woof!*

Stephen Bridges (9)
Badsey First School, Badsey

Superman

My brother is Superman jumping on the sofa.
'Will you stop!' shouted Mum.
My brother didn't listen.
I joined in too.
'Weeeeeeeeeee, I am Superman!'
Mum came back in and we got in so much trouble.

Sam Dean (9)
Badsey First School, Badsey

Harley And Me

Harley went on a walk but instead of me taking him for a walk
He takes me for a walk.
We've only had him for a couple of months.
He has settled in nicely so we have had a great time.
Harley barks and barks at people, he does not stop.
Whoops!

Adam Ballard (9)
Badsey First School, Badsey

Snowflakes On The Wall

Snowflakes on the wall,
Wind blows, snowflakes go,
Where do snowflakes go?
I don't know.

Molly Morris (8)
Badsey First School, Badsey

Poem

I've got soaked!
I got soaked because my big coat got soaked.
The good thing was there was a shop
And that was where I stopped and swapped,
So now I have a cloak
And a man has my coat.

Immy Smith (8)
Badsey First School, Badsey

Winter Butterfly

Snowflakes falling gracefully from the sky,
Dancing patterns like a beautiful butterfly.
Snowflakes spinning, twirling, whirling,
Sparkling feathers icily floating and dropping
Gently onto the snow.

Rebecca Phillips (8)
Badsey First School, Badsey

Monkeys Eat Bananas

Monkeys eat bananas,
But they don't wear pyjamas.
Monkeys swing from tree to tree,
They can't talk but they are cheeky.

Oliver Hampton (8)
Badsey First School, Badsey

My Hamster

Fat and greedy
Cute and cuddly
Quick and sharp
Night-time hunter
Beware!

Joe Green (9)
Brockhampton Primary School, Worcester

My Sister

My sister is sly and sneaky
My sister is weird and freaky
Nicking biscuits out the tin
Throwing food in the bin
Going to bed at 12 o'clock
Closing the door with a great big lock
Having lunch with fingers, no fork
Chatting on the carpet, talk, talk, talk
We are going to the sweet shop, yeah, yeah, yeah
What is my sister going to do today?
She bought some sweets, 15 pounds worth
When I bought a drink to quench my thirst
This is what my sister's like
If you see her tell her to get on her bike!

Brooke Stancliffe (9)
Brockhampton Primary School, Worcester

Mums And Dads

Are always . . .
Cleaning,
Cooking,
Sleeping,
Watching telly,
Reading books,
Shopping,
Planning days out,
But most of all they love their kids.

Laura Wilks (9)
Brockhampton Primary School, Worcester

My Brother

My brother is always squabbling, whingeing, moaning and fighting.
He hates me, football, rugby, everything I like.
He likes motorbikes, cuddles,
Pretty much everything I hate.
I am so glad you don't have a brother like mine!

Tom Baker (9)
Brockhampton Primary School, Worcester

My Cousin, Barnaby

Long bristly hair
Longer than a bear
Longer than a giraffe sitting on that bear,
'Look!' A hare ran up the giraffe and the bear,
But it's longer than that!

Angus Gibbs (9)
Brockhampton Primary School, Worcester

Fear

Fear is the one,
It screams at you,
'Don't do it!' it cries,
If you conquer Fear,
The voice will stop.

Tom Hutchinson (11)
Brockhampton Primary School, Worcester

A Penguin In Space

A penguin in space
Is so bright
He likes to move
In lots of light.

A penguin from space
Is like a penguin from Earth
But he is on Venus
He likes to eat from birth.

A penguin in space
Who likes aliens from Mars
The aliens are so scary,
The penguin is too heavy to go behind bars.

A penguin from space
Who likes to meet stars
He drives a vehicle
His very old Dad owed him a car.

Morgan Yarrington-Bull (9)
Burlish Park Primary School, Stourport-on-Severn

My Life As A TV

The door opened and they came in!
I'd been on that table, unused for months,
Doing nothing, waiting for that door to open.
When it opened I knew that the torture had begun,
He picked the remote up
And turned me on.

My mouth booming unspoken words and noises,
My eyes being used for despicable soaps,
Disgusting documentaries
And worst of all, the chaotic kids' channels.
I loath to be flicked through like that.

I had a problem that they didn't know,
One of my buttons was going way too slow.
They never used that record button,
Because they were on time to watch,
'Merlin', 'Doctor Who' and 'X Factor'.

I started to get a speaker ache,
I could say nothing at all,
Not a single word,
But those weren't my worries,
Oh I had bigger problems,
Like the record button being pressed!

It didn't work,
He shouted, 'Dad, the TV's broke!'
My motherboard froze in fear of the bin,
My screen turned into a black cave of darkness,
My speakers into a continuous buzzing bee
And my remote friend exploded.

Two days later,
A TV repair man looked at me,
He said to Dad,
'You need a new TV!'

The day after,
I went to the skip with Dad's old shoes,
I went in a bin called
Re . . . cyc . . . ling.

All that happened then till now was a blur,
All I know is that I'm a humble telephone,
In a shop, ready to go.

Thomas Allen (10)
Burlish Park Primary School, Stourport-on-Severn

The Shak

And . . . does he attack?
Oh, he's got sharp teeth,
Sharp nails on his paws
Oh, his name is Keeth
And he's got big jaws.

And . . . what colour is he?
Oh, he's brown,
And a bit of blue,
He likes to frown
And he says, 'Moo.'

And . . . who are his relatives?
Oh one's a cat
Another is a shark,
Third one is a Dak
And the last is a Cark.

And . . .who are his enemies?
Oh humans and Boons
Oh Mumans as well
Also Coons.

And . . . what are his hobbies?
Eating *humans!*
And I think I don't want to give any more information.
Oh please try,
I will give you some cake,
Or some pie,
That's what I'll make.

Daniel Stokes (9)
Burlish Park Primary School, Stourport-on-Severn

My Life As A Car

The garage door opened!
Yet another day began.
My doors flung open,
In flooded the cold, vicious wind.
Huge black shadows came again
'Ouch! That was extremely painful!'
As my seats were roughly sat on.

But where to? I wondered,
Children screaming, excited
About their day out.
'Not long now,'
Was all Dad kept saying!
Bumpy roads, sharp bends,
The dreaded traffic lights!

Feeling warm, a sudden *hissss!*
Was I breaking down?
Yes - my engine stopped,
We waited and waited then . . .
Bang! Clunk! Clatter!
Hooked up to the rescue truck,
And on the move again.
To the garage, fixed up quick
Then back home to my quiet garage
Snug, warm and finally happy.
What an adventure!

Sarah Daniels (10)
Burlish Park Primary School, Stourport-on-Severn

The Clock

My hands go round my numbered face,
I always attract attention to people passing by,
People look at me and they know their fate,
If they are a minute late.

At 10.14 for goodness' sake,
When will it be playtime break?
At 3.15 they all go home
And leave me here all on my own.

Matthew Adams (10)
Burlish Park Primary School, Stourport-on-Severn

The Monster

And . . . what was it like?
Oh, it's scary and fat
Bumped and spike-eared and groany.
It's hairy and spotty
And likes to eat a fat pony.

And . . . where does it live?
Oh, in comets and spaceships
And in craters and in deep black holes.
In pulsars and sheep dips
And it lives in the North Pole.

And . . . what does it eat?
Oh, boiling rocks and fish fins
And X-rays and moon dust.
Then rotten meat and spiky pins
And steaming lava and space crust.

And . . . who are its enemies?
Oh, Jupiter and Mars
And Neptune and Mercury
Wig wags and chocolate bars
And his worst enemy is Venus.

And . . . and . . . what does it wear?
Nothing!
It's bare!

Grace Baldwin (9)
Burlish Park Primary School, Stourport-on-Severn

My Life As A Car

I have just been born,
My wheels are being put on,
Then I am being taken to be sold.
A few days later I am bought and someone takes me away.
I am scared that he might throw me away and leave,
But he drives me everywhere, to the shop, even to Oxford University!
When he goes on holiday I stay at the airport for two months.
When he comes back he drives me to the scrapyard and this is the end of my life as a car.

Mark Westcott (10)
Burlish Park Primary School, Stourport-on-Severn

My Life As A Table

The solid, stiff door slammed wide open
And the children flooded in, they were nasty,
They sat solidly on my poor friend, the chair
And then slapped me with a hard, hasty book.
I felt truly sorry for the book,
However, I was hurt badly,
My side was throbbing madly!
It was worse than a fish being caught on a spiky, sharp hook.
Oh, how I hated the children and their big books.

The most horrible part of my day is when
Children draw rude pictures on me
And stick gross chewing gum on me, 'Yuck.'
It's every table's nightmare when an evil child does this.
It is so hard to scrub off when I clean myself slowly.
However, there is one part of the day which I enjoy,
It is when the children get hungry,
Because they place their plates on me, they are warm,
This is a sensational feeling.
It tickles my tummy,
It warms me in the ice-cold classroom.
How I adore this feeling.

Although I always have a rough start,
I end up with a great finish!

Phoebe Francis (10)
Burlish Park Primary School, Stourport-on-Severn

My Life As A Shoe

There I waited in the shop, standing tall, waiting to be chosen.
Suddenly a warm hand grabbed me and took me to the till.
There she sat, my new owner.
As the shopkeeper bundled me into a cold, dark box I felt the shop slipping away.

Two weeks gone, she opened the box and I knew that her fat cheesy feet were going to go in me.
My nightmare was about to begin.
As she walked on me it was agony.
Five months later I was torn apart and it was time for the bin.

Sophie Condon (10)
Burlish Park Primary School, Stourport-on-Severn

My Life As A Door

I am standing there waiting to be opened,
I block the light between rooms.
People twist my arm to open me,
I am a portal from one room to the other.

I see lots of people come past every day,
They are strangers to me.
I have a key to keep me locked all the time
And stop the trespassers coming through.

The postman comes and feeds me post,
It tastes like postcodes and stamps.
I drop it out my back for people to collect,
They open the envelope and read inside.

When my family goes on holiday, I get bored.
I gather dust and need polishing.
When they get back they twist my arm.
I feel a tickle like I used to.

When I get old my skin wrinkles and my paint cracks.
When someone's angry they slam me shut!
'Ow,' I say but they don't hear.
I try not to creak when my family's asleep.
I am the door, the key to the outside world.

Liam Shelton (10)
Burlish Park Primary School, Stourport-on-Severn

The Hairy Thing

But how does it walk?
It bounces on its belly
Rolls around like a big nelly!

But what does it eat?
Solid rocks, sun eggs and super smelly socks.

But where does it live?
Dirty holes with the moles.

But what's his hobby?
Chewing toe nails, eating dust,
And sitting on other creatures as chairs.

Safronne Lee (9)
Burlish Park Primary School, Stourport-on-Severn

Computer Mouse

Every day I get frantically banged,
It's not the monitor's fault or mine.
It's the computer's fault, he's too slow.
I still get banged and shaken but there's only one thing I do
Over and over again.

When I get wiggled it tickles my belly.
I then find I am moving, it makes me feel funny,
I get loved all the time,
And it gives me a sign that I am loved and that's all I need to know.

The energy zips through me and lights me up.
Suddenly I get pressed,
She heaves my head down and it hurts.
Life as a computer mouse is very dull.
I just wish that I would break so I could be a fabulous garden rake!

It's now months later,
I wanted to be a garden rake but instead was a jumbled up pile just resting in the bin.
So there I lie, my life is still dim!
I once was loved but now by the bin.
I am old and no place to live.
Times have moved on and so have I.

Jordan Rigby (10)
Burlish Park Primary School, Stourport-on-Severn

Unknown Monster

Far, far away in an unknown galaxy,
Something wobbled across the planet like a jelly.
It bounced on the floor, it bounced off the wall.
And what did it eat? Nothing at all!
Far, far away in an unknown galaxy,
A green, slimy alien was climbing a tree.
It jumped in a car and chased a star.
And what did it eat? A Milky Way bar!
Far, far away in an unknown galaxy,
An alien asked me to tea.
And what did it eat?
'Oh no, it ate me!'

Kieran Russell (10)
Burlish Park Primary School, Stourport-on-Severn

My Life As A Carrot

Lying lazily in a cardboard box, when suddenly he picks me up!
Leaving my brothers and sisters behind, I become scared.
Thrown in the basket my journey begins,
First the milk, then the cheese,
Followed by a Mars bar and a Barbie doll.
I am now at the bottom of the shopping basket.
Suffocating in a plastic bag,
He throws me into the boot of his car
And slams the door tightly with no chance of escape.

Finally, I arrive at his house and the nightmare begins.
Pulled from the bag, then slung on the chopping board,
I am now face to face with the enemy!
First chop, my tuft of hair is sliced away!
Next he slices through my feet, legs, tummy and head!
Tumbling, terrified, into the bubbling, boiling water,
Can I miss the saucepan?

Just as I thought it couldn't get any worse,
I am scooped from the saucepan and lay on the plate.
Jabbed hungrily by the fork, which kind of tickled a bit,
I know my time is up,
My life as a carrot is no more . . .

Emily Jones (10)
Burlish Park Primary School, Stourport-on-Severn

My Life As A Tree

The curtains open as I gaze upon a new day
With the birds tweeting for me to awake,
Leaves rustling in the breeze,
A friendly face gazes upon me,
Which tells me they've come to play.

A squirrel runs up my spine,
Tickles me as he goes.
Children play on the open field,
Then come dashing for shelter at my feet,
While I take my afternoon shower.
As the light turns out and sun goes down,
I wait for another day to come.

Jasmine Canty (10)
Burlish Park Primary School, Stourport-on-Severn

My Life As A Bed

My life is pretty boring if you ask me,
I'm slept on and I wait all day long alone,
Then I'm slept on again,
When I'm used it hurts my back
And when I'm not used I'm all alone.

I like it when my clothes are washed and I get clean fresh ones,
My life is as boring as a slave's,
All one does is work,
All I do is be lonely,
The worst is when people bounce on me,
It's so, so painful.

The one thing I hate is that people don't appreciate me.
They just stamp on me,
It's like they don't know I'm alive,
I bet they couldn't last one day holding me up at night!
The humans don't know how hard it is being a bed.

I love it when they tuck me in on a morning,
They make me neat and crease free,
I also love the patterns on my clothes they put on me.

Alex Rose (10)
Burlish Park Primary School, Stourport-on-Severn

My Life As A Football

I have been in that bag for weeks,
Bored; I just want to be played with.
So the kids can tickle me with their boots,
The kids are playing next week,
That could be my day.

Then Saturday comes,
The coach picks up the bag.
I am the first ball out,
I feel so happy, today's the day.

The referee puts me on the spot.
He blows the whistle and they start to play.
The kids' boots tickle so much I just can't stop,
Jumping into the net.

Bradley Worton (10)
Burlish Park Primary School, Stourport-on-Severn

My Life As A Horse

The stable door flung open and in they came.
They thumped the saddle on my back.
I got so excited, but then I could hear them say,
'You're too big for that pony, we will put him up for sale.'
Suddenly tears were dripping down my neck.
I didn't want to be sold.

Left in my stable, all alone,
She didn't come and see me for days.
Then I heard the rustling of the stones,
It was the horse box with its door down.
I thought I was going to a show.

What is going on? I thought.
After a long drive we arrived.
They wound down the horse box door.
Where was I?
A voice whispered to me, 'Welcome to your new home.'
I was so scared.

I had a wonderful life with both families,
But I'll have a new family soon.

Izzy Prescott (10)
Burlish Park Primary School, Stourport-on-Severn

My Dog Life

Pouncing around with my silly floppy siblings
But suddenly some strange looking things came into my house.
A bratty looking child and a tall man.
My owner picked me up and put me in a van.

I was scared, I wanted to cry
But before I knew it we were at a place called Stourport.
Arriving at some sort of house, a short lady picked me up and cuddled me.

When I got to know them, they were great.
I love my owners,
They even gave me a name, Molly.

I do not know what I was thinking, that my new owners were horrid,
I so take that back.

Meghan Turner (11)
Burlish Park Primary School, Stourport-on-Severn

My Life As A Homework Diary

Once I'm opened I don't want to be closed.
I'm ecstatic when people talk to me,
But I know deep down inside,
They're not nice people because day in, day out
People write on me and it hurts with great pain.
Their comments and homework they write on me
Are the only friends I've got,
Without me you'd be lost in your daily routine.
There are hundreds of me in school
But I am unique to every pupil.
I would like a sense of style but to look at me I'm quite plain.
Just remember I help people in many ways like
Reminding you of homework, clubs, house points
And many more useful things.
I also hold lots of autographs of teachers and parents,
So I must be popular.
I start off clean and tidy but by the end of July I'm all old and tatty.
I wish people would just love and care for me, even if it's for a day.
I'm always in and out of my owner's bag.
Why can't something adventurous happen to me?

Amy Breakwell (11)
Burlish Park Primary School, Stourport-on-Severn

The Splodge

And . . . what does it look like?
Oh it is 85,697 years old
It has gel everywhere
It has 15 spikes on its back, even on its face.

And what does it eat?
It eats creepy-crawlies
And anything that is in its way.
Children are super treats!

And . . . is it friendly?
No it not friendly at all
It is horrifying.

And . . . and . . . what does it wear?
Nothing apart from super smelly socks.

Kieran O'Neill (9)
Burlish Park Primary School, Stourport-on-Severn

My Day As A Pair Of Tights

The drawer was yanked open
And a familiar face appeared.
Today was the day, I could feel it,
Out again from the dark, yes I was right,
She picked me up and put me on,
First the one leg then the next.

Running down the stairs two at a time,
She scraped me badly on both knees,
My fine delicate weave stretched to its limit,
I had heard about times like this,
Little girls who wear me,
I'd heard that they never end well!

My fears were realised,
When we made our way to the park;
As she climbed along the climbing frame,
Twisting and turning I knew I couldn't hold out.
The holes began to appear,
Holes too big to mend,
The only place left for me was the bin.

Megan Oliver (11)
Burlish Park Primary School, Stourport-on-Severn

Planets And Aliens

On the sun blazing hot,
There is an alien with a spot.
On the moon,
Astronauts zoom,
The alien going, 'Boom!'
On the moon,
A fat alien is eating the craters to make them bigger and deeper.
On Venus
Live a mad fat alien,
He was made out of chocolate,
Also he tries eating himself.
On Neptune
There lives an alien who look just like . . . *you!*

Shannon Bradley (9)
Burlish Park Primary School, Stourport-on-Severn

The Fan

Here I am, stuck back here,
I'm only here, chattering with my ear,
My back on rough hard wood,
They chucked me here with a thud,
Back then my life was quite fine
And then the winter came again.

Oh how I hate the winter,
I've got such a bad splinter,
I hear the stormy thunder and pouring rain,
I wish the fire would come with a flame,
I hope the summer comes soon,
I used to feel as if I was on the moon.

Eventually the summer is here,
I no longer live in fear,
I've been taken out and waved around,
At least my feelings have been found,
The warm heat on my belly
When they're sitting watching telly,
Oh how I love the summer.

Lucy Rollins (10)
Burlish Park Primary School, Stourport-on-Severn

How Is The Sun Today?

I have been looking so hard behind the clouds,
To see if the big happy sun is out,
I have looked right, left, and all about,
'I am too tired and annoyed with the rain!'
I heard the sun shout, meanwhile the puddles were gone,
Then again, I was looking so hard
Behind the clouds,
Just in case the big happy sun is out,
'Those puddles taste delicious,'
It was the sun in all,
Just in front of my eyes was a big yellow ball!
It was in the sky saying,
'I am so glad to be the sun.'

Ellie Blaze (10)
Burlish Park Primary School, Stourport-on-Severn

The Blob

And . . . what can it see?
It can see millions of miles from Venus to Mars,
It can see in the dark.
Its eyes roll in its glowing blob
It can see all the way to Lickhill Park.

What does it look like?
Oh, it's big, it's fat, and it runs around like a bat,
It's round like a lump of jelly
And it also looks like a mat.

And . . . what does it smell like?
It's stinky, it's smelly,
It smells like a really smelly sock.

And . . . what is its job?
Its job is to gobble little children just like you.
Juicy tender flesh!

And . . . where does it live?
It lives on Neptune with Bob, Mob, Sob, Frog
And Flippaty-Flob.

Daniel Roby (9)
Burlish Park Primary School, Stourport-on-Severn

My Dinner Lady

At 12.25, the dinner bell rings,
'It's lunchtime, it's lunchtime!' she tunefully sings,
It's Miss Lunar I'm talking about of course,
Her back all creaky, her voice quite hoarse.

I think she's an alien, it's easy to observe,
The way her body miraculously swerves,
Her hands quiver sadistically and are slimy all over
And her feet are flat as if by a steamroller.

My dinner lady's an alien don't you see?
It's a queer thing to say . . . naturally.
This is the end, the bell violently clatters,
But I've had a lovely dinner, that's all that matters.

Jessica McPhee (9)
Burlish Park Primary School, Stourport-on-Severn

Weird Alien

On the Earth,
Made of rock,
There lives an alien
Who got a shock.

On the sun
Blazing hot,
There lives an alien
With one big spot.

On the moon
Astronauts zoom,
There lives an alien,
The alien in his room going *boom*.

On Mars
Full of Mars bars
There lives an alien
Driving lots of big red cars.

And . . . and what is he like?
Funny, stinky, smelly, silly, small and cool.

Callum Parry (9)
Burlish Park Primary School, Stourport-on-Severn

My Life As A Keyboard

Someone's pressed a switch,
Suddenly a surge of electricity comes flying through me,
People are poking me, gosh it tickles,
No matter how tired I am, I always have to perform,
It's such a hard life.

Some kind people play with me gently,
Whereas others poke and pinch,
The notes come out as clear as a bell,
Some pitched high and some are low,
I do get bored with my life as a keyboard.

All the fun dies down as the switch gets flicked off,
And I drift peacefully off to sleep.

Stephanie Whaile (10)
Burlish Park Primary School, Stourport-on-Severn

Aliens, Aliens, Aliens

Aliens, aliens, aliens,
They live on a planet called Bailens,
They're green, mean, slobby sailors,
And they are always failures.

Aliens, aliens, aliens,
The naughty, angry aliens,
They never smile like a star,
And they never speak Zaliens.

Aliens, aliens, aliens,
How big will they grow?
They never laugh like aliens,
And they are awesome pros.

Aliens, aliens, aliens,
They're always pale pink,
They're always craliens,
They single blink,
With their only eye,
Aliens, aliens, aliens.

Louisa Garland (9)
Burlish Park Primary School, Stourport-on-Severn

My Life As A Sharpener

The moment they opened that case,
I saw the sun smiling at me,
I smiled back, me and the sun are best friends,
When the sharpenings are in me it hurts!

After a while when the pencil was down to blunt,
He was put inside me,
The pencil didn't like me,
I didn't like him,
Then when they picked me up they started sharpening.

It hurts so bad
It scratched me, gave me bruises,
I got loads of cuts,
When I am broken I have to go in a horrid place . . .
The bin . . .

Amy Lewis (11)
Burlish Park Primary School, Stourport-on-Severn

The Sun, The Sun

We are hot at 14,000,000 degrees,
I am a star, never go near me
Because I am very hot
And I could melt your spaceship
But in June I shine on London.

I give you light and heat
I am a big ball of hot gas and I am spotty
My spots are called sunspots
One day I will use up all of the gas and die.

I line up in space with the Earth and moon
And make an eclipse.
Some of me is very cool
But my inside is very, very hot
I am the centre of the universe
I am the biggest star.

If you look at me I can damage your eyes
Lots of planets orbit me, my favourite is Mars
I am sometimes hotter than boiling water.

Olivia Turner (9)
Burlish Park Primary School, Stourport-on-Severn

In Another Galaxy

In another galaxy
There is another Earth
With purple-skinned maniacs
Who eat a meal called Parth.

In another galaxy
They have a moon called Toon
With living slimy blobs
They all have nineteen moons.

In another galaxy
The sun is very small
With used-to-the-heat aliens
Those aliens are extremely tall.

Emily Rose Carrier (10)
Burlish Park Primary School, Stourport-on-Severn

My Life As A Chair

'Ring, ring!' shouted Bell that woke me up,
Children dashed up the ramp,
A child picked me at last to put me next to his desk, and sat on me,
I felt warm and happy but wait, he got off me and left the room,
Where was he going?
The class always went out leaving us to freeze,
It was an entire 15 minutes before he came back with the class.
He sat down on me again!
Boy that felt warm, I wished I could jump for joy!
The class swapped over as usual but my friend, Desk,
Got pushed away.
I could not move then I got picked up as high as the window
Looking down at the ground.
I realised I was going to another desk, the lesson went on and on.
After she got off and left us again I heard noise outside
We could not see outside because we couldn't move!
Screaming and running was happening on all sides!
Looking around and wondering again when it was going to stop.
As soon as Bell rang the children came in like mindless zombies.

Dylan Moreton (10)
Burlish Park Primary School, Stourport-on-Severn

The Green Tree

Standing tall in all weathers,
Rain, snow and sun.
Watching children climb up me,
Having lots of fun.
It tickles and tickles me,
Oh I am a popular tree.
My leaves are green, gold and brown,
One morning a leaf falls,
Autumn's coming, I frown.

Green buds appear all over me,
I've grown into a leafy tree!
I hear children coming out,
Happily watching them playing about.
Come and play on me,
I'm a popular tree!

Charlotte Voysey (10)
Burlish Park Primary School, Stourport-on-Severn

The M1 A2 Abrams' First Battle

The desert sweated in the noon heat,
As the Abrams crawled across the sand.
It heard the distant growl of its enemy the T72
It began to sprint across the swirling desert,
Eager to fight its first battle.

It climbed the mountainous sand dune,
And scanned the desert looking for its foe,
There below it was 2 o'clock, a crowd of T72s
Lurking in the shadows.
The tank growled its challenge as it lurched forward,
The T72's turret turned to stare at it.

The Abrams screamed its excitement as it slid down the sand dune,
Its machine gun spitting a hail of bullets.
The Abrams dodged a shell
Its main gun turned to glare at the T72,
It released a devastating shell, turning it to a smoking wreck.
The rest of the enemy fled like an Olympic running team,
The Abrams stood proudly surveying its first victory.

Joe Waldron (10)
Burlish Park Primary School, Stourport-on-Severn

My Life As A Rubber

My cardboard cover was slipped off
The girl picked me up, I was terrified.
I was kept in a totally different place to all the others,
Although I knew what was coming next.

I was lowered to the paper.
Next I was being rubbed.
Getting smaller all the time.

Like all rubbers,
One day we all go,
Go to the bins,
I'm still big but one day it will be my turn
For the bins!

Seona Davies (10)
Burlish Park Primary School, Stourport-on-Severn

My Life As A Football

The door to the cupboard opened
Would they pick me?
As their hands came towards me
I stretched myself forward.

Yes they picked me!
I am a football.
They carried me
To the pitch.

We were off.
I was passed from child to child
Gliding through the air
Rolling on the ground.

Until my sides felt like
They would explode
As the game finished I landed
In the back of the net.

Ben Napthine (11)
Burlish Park Primary School, Stourport-on-Severn

My Life As A Tyre

I started my life as a tree,
The bendy black stuff they extracted from me,
In a container we were put
As we knew this was just our luck.

To a factory we did go,
To make our bodies not stiff but flow,
We were made into a mould
From this people were told
To buy us and make it good
To drive on roads, just so we could.

I didn't get dizzy although I'm round,
I just make my vehicle grip to the ground,
To some I'm grippy, to some I'm slick
Whatever the use I will make them stick,
To all my uses I will make it safe,
As on my tyres you are so safe.

Emma Parsons (11)
Burlish Park Primary School, Stourport-on-Severn

My Life As A Computer

Patiently, I am turned on.
It feels like it is a brand new day,
Which I always love,
Even though when I load I go slowly.
Then the human shouts, 'Come on,'
That makes me feel sad.

As I'm being used I feel really useful and brainy,
Then I get loved like you humans do,
But there is one problem, the charger,
It hurts when the electric is pumped into me.
Sometimes I get hotter when I am overused.

As my owner goes to shut me down, I know I will not be used for another week,
Now I have to be plugged in by the charger,
I realise it will hurt,
I still have to go through the same things every week.

Harry Deacon (10)
Burlish Park Primary School, Stourport-on-Severn

My Life As A Sun

I like being a sun but I get extremely bored, watching the world go around.
Sitting in space day in, day out.
But the sparkly stars keep me company.
People look happy when I shine down on them.

I absolutely hate it when the clouds stop my beams because everybody is sad and dull.
The stars' friend, the moon, gets in the way when I am shining down on Earth.
I hate the moon, he is so boring.
At night he shines brighter than me!

Earth is a very fantastic place to be.
I wish I was a person, dancing around all the time.
There is lots of water, not much land.
I see lots of boats sailing out on the sea, some are very big and some are very small.
This is the life of being a sun.

Megan Lloyd (10)
Burlish Park Primary School, Stourport-on-Severn

T-Shirt Personification

I sleep in your wardrobe,
Nowhere to be seen,
When you open the door I shout,
'Help me, oh please!'
I'm old and scruffy but you can still wear me.

When you wear me I feel alive!
I just want to dance and play
And have fun with you all day!
'Please, oh please, get me out to play!'
I beg, I plead and I'll do anything!

I feel warm when I'm in the wash,
The whooshing water waves me about.
I like that, but I want to play with you!
I love the iron upon my chest,
The warm blade of iron,
Smoothing my creased fabrics out.

Ryan Harper (10)
Burlish Park Primary School, Stourport-on-Severn

My Life As A Gym Bar

They all come in after a hard day of working at school,
Waiting to come on me, the bars,
The children make me laugh when they speak to me,
I am happy being used to help them.

My friend is the vault who hates children,
There is also the beam who likes children walking on him,
The floor loves children's hot feet keeping her warm in the winter.

There are about a thousand children that use me per week,
I get cramp sometimes by being used too many times,
Though I don't mind it as long as I have company.

They bend me and they tread on me, those heavy children,
I dread the warm up because they have two children on the bar at once,
I know that one day soon I will break and that will be the end of me.

I am proud to be what I am,
The bars.

Danielle O'Neill (10)
Burlish Park Primary School, Stourport-on-Severn

The Blinker

And . . . what is it like?
Oh, it's terrifying and skeletal, warlike and old.
It's smelly and groany and lacy and thick-headed and bony.

And . . . where does it live?
Oh, in comets and very old spaceships and pulsars and black holes.
In skulls and Mars bars and fat poles.

And . . . what does it eat?
Oh, fat legs and plums and moon crust and fat.
Then spaceships and drums.

And . . . who are its friends?
Oh, ponkers and donkers and thinkers and flurpers.
Then florkars and borkers and slonkers and bonkers.

And . . . who are its enemies?
Oh, swashbucklers and binks and surgers and centuryks.
Also zober blobbers and dinks and okkotkays and smellkas.

Ben Evans (9)
Burlish Park Primary School, Stourport-on-Severn

My Life As A Football

I love it when they pick me up ready for a football match.
After years of waiting it's time they put me on the floor.
I can't wait for the kick off.

Finally the time has come for a brilliant game.
The whistle blows.

Oh no, they've studded me, ouch! What was that?
Oh no, a hole in me.
This is bad news, they can't mend me, and it's time for the bin.
They chuck me in the bin, soon a player comes in,
He picks me up out of the bin.

He's fixed me, he brings me outside and kicks me.
I don't go down, unbelievably I get put in the cupboard ready for the next game.

I thought I was going to be put in the bin forever, well I'm not.
I hope I will never get studded again.

Ellis Troth (11)
Burlish Park Primary School, Stourport-on-Severn

My Life As A Computer Mouse

It's a blistering hot day and the family will be back in a minute,
Happily they'll run in and put their hand over me, squashing me painfully,
Soon the boy is going to play on boring 'Club Penguin',
I can imagine his hand is on top of me as quick as a bullet!

It's not all bad and I'm not exaggerating because when I fall off the table
I bungee jump, even better, they pick me up carefully, lovely.
I'm not moaning but I hate it when they scroll my scroll wheel because it's like having your delicate ears pulled off.

Being a mouse is like being in a prison cell because you are trapped
And it's the stupid wire's fault!
So now I can't go anywhere like I'm in jail. Poor old me!

But like I said it's not all that bad because I get to speak to Computer quite often,
We chat about how boring Computer's life is.
And that, my friend is the life of me, The Computer Mouse.

Bradley Mason (10)
Burlish Park Primary School, Stourport-on-Severn

Another Galaxy

In another galaxy aliens play tig
Far, far away.

In another galaxy aliens fight
Fighting for survival
Lasers strapped to a kite.

In another galaxy aliens sleep
When they get woken up
They cry and they weep.

In another galaxy aliens eat
I don't really know what
But I think gooey meat.

In another galaxy aliens talk
Some gibberish language
They use multicoloured chalk.

Alex Jones (9)
Burlish Park Primary School, Stourport-on-Severn

Aliens In My Pie

One evening at tea,
I excused myself for a wee,
I came back down with a curious eye,
Thinking I had an alien in my pie.

I tried to take a bite,
But my face turned white,
I did not know why
But I knew there was an alien in my pie.

I ran outside,
And I hid under the slide
I knew I could die,
Because I saw an alien in my pie.

Nathan David Farmer (9)
Burlish Park Primary School, Stourport-on-Severn

Goodbye Bob

Down in the crater,
Lives an alien called Bob,
He is a spotty purple blob,
He lives in space,
With a blood-red face.

Down in a crater,
Bob dances a crazy dance,
He twists his legs and jigs and prances,
Without thinking,
He is sinking,
Into melted chocolate,
Goodbye Bob.

Jessica Barrett (10)
Burlish Park Primary School, Stourport-on-Severn

The Dining Dinner Blob

Each evening Miss Doodacot puts up her feet,
While munching and crunching a gooey piece of meat.
Tired and weary from a tough day at work.
She was sure that those Earthlings would send her berserk.

At 12 o'clock she served a load of glop,
With a spoonful of snot.
Well, all the young aliens loved this stuff
But there was one rather big puff.

When all of a sudden the lunch bell would ring,
Why, Miss Doodacot would fling her things and say,
'Hurry along my little dumplings!'

Georgia Little (10)
Burlish Park Primary School, Stourport-on-Severn

Planet Doo-Bee-Doo

On the planet Doo-Bee-Doo
People are waiting just for you!
The colour is green and blue
So why not come to Doo-Bee-Doo?

It orbits Mars
And has lots of cars
So we can travel to the stars!

On the planet Doo-Bee-Doo
You can go to the old wild zoo,
There are so many things to do
So come along to Doo-Bee-Doo!

Chloe Davies (9)
Burlish Park Primary School, Stourport-on-Severn

The Zooper Blooper

And . . . what does it eat?
Moon eggs, Mars grit, hot rocks, comet fumes and human feet.

And . . . where does it live?
Craters with his mates, moon rakers and spaceships.

And . . . what does it eat?
Moon rocks, sun eggs, comet fumes and human feet.

And . . . what does it look like?
Fluffy, hairy, tall, scruffy and wobbly.

And . . . what does it wear?
An old pair of underwear!

Jordan Rowbottom (10)
Burlish Park Primary School, Stourport-on-Severn

My Life As A Television

It's dark in the box but when they open it the light floods in,
At the touch of a button I leap to life,
I sit in the corner of the lounge,
They always know I'm there for them,
They say I'm as flat as a pancake, I know that's true,
It hurts when they pull the plug on me,
Friendless, I sit around all day,
I get spooked when I notice them looking deep into my eyes,
Different channels change my mood,
Lonely, when they're out, I go to sleep.

Sam Turbutt (10)
Burlish Park Primary School, Stourport-on-Severn

Space Race

Around Mars, Venus, Pluto and the moon,
The space race is underway.
USA and USSR battling to get the first rocket rumbling out of its stand.
Around the planets, past the sun,
Where is the moon? There it is,
Next to the Earth and the sun.

Dan Rowley (10)
Burlish Park Primary School, Stourport-on-Severn

The Famous Spin

Up in the air there is a big black puddle.
Up in the air the stars get in a muddle.
The Earth and moon orbit the sun.
The sun is the biggest star.
The Earth spins on its axis all 24 hours.
The sun uses up all its power all day.
The sun will dry up in five billion years.
The Earth spins extremely slowly in a whole day.
That's how the Earth, sun and moon are the famous three.

Daniel Bell (9)
Burlish Park Primary School, Stourport-on-Severn

My Life As A Saddle

I sit for hours on my saddle stand,
And then the fun begins . . .
She picks me up and places me on a warm, soft, furry back.
This is my very favourite place.
She grabs hold of me and pulls my straps tight.
The feeling of excitement is building as I know what to expect.
Where will our adventures take us today?
The common? The old railway? Jumping in the menage?
Wherever Lucy and Thunder take me, we will have fun together.

Lucy Elliott (11)
Burlish Park Primary School, Stourport-on-Severn

Miss Goggle

Each evening Miss Goggle went out to play and stayed out all day.
While munching and crunching a gooey piece of meat
She sat on the sofa and put up her feet.

Next day Miss Goggle drew some spikes
And fell down her long extraordinary pipe.

Miss Goggle was well-behaved and extremely well paid.
She was an alien who came out of space
And won the greatest running race.

Lucy McLatchy (9)
Burlish Park Primary School, Stourport-on-Severn

Standing On A Planet

Standing on a planet,
In another time zone.
There's a bright, sunny garden,
Where a cat lies curled.

Standing on a planet,
Looking at the dazzling stars,
I see an astronaut
Near another star.

Elsie Cole (9)
Burlish Park Primary School, Stourport-on-Severn

Horrible Aliens

Horrible aliens, one trillion miles away,
They couldn't possibly come to Earth could they?
Hundreds of aliens scattered everywhere,
They're asleep half of the day so they can't go anywhere.

For dinner they gobble up snoz rags
And to finish off they all have a spoonful of snot,
To fill their tummies to the top,
But after that if they're still hungry they'll tear their friends to eat!

Ben Voyce (10)
Burlish Park Primary School, Stourport-on-Severn

The Solar System

First in the line comes Mercury and Venus,
These are the closest planets to the sun.
Earth, Mars and Jupiter come after that pair
And Earth is the only planet with living things on.
Saturn, Uranus and Neptune are last in the queue
And are officially the coldest planets.
The sun is first in the solar system but it is not a planet,
It is a star though and it's made of hydrogen and helium.

Becky Edwards (9)
Burlish Park Primary School, Stourport-on-Severn

My Life As A Book

I was swung open like a door.
I heard someone laughing, I felt a horrible pain!
Then I realised I was being ripped to pieces.
When I thought it was the end the person stopped, it was a relief.
But when I was too busy cheering I was shut and lunged into the bin.
I was all on my own, I was very upset, when suddenly someone picked me up and took me to a new home and looked after me.
I am so happy now, today is my best day ever!

Ryan Cadwallader (10)
Burlish Park Primary School, Stourport-on-Severn

Miss Gogglot The Alien

Each evening Miss Gogglot puts up her feet,
While munching and crunching a gooey piece of meat,
In the hours with the Earthlings
She uses her tentacles to serve things
And then takes out her purse to collect the payment she deserves.
When she gets home she flings off her clothes, picks up a rose
And starts dancing around with a wicked pose,
But watch out for her stinking toes.

Megan Bush (9)
Burlish Park Primary School, Stourport-on-Severn

Teacher

I sit straight in class, but she still picks on me.
I clean up the classroom,
I polish it and all, then I spell the word cat!
I get it wrong and she shouts at me!
She tells me, 'Sit down in the naughty corner, I'm cross with you!'
So I do it of course,
It makes me feel bored, school's supposed to be fun not rubbish.
School should be cool!
So I say, 'That's enough.'
I stand on the table, I shout at her.
I tell her who's boss, 'Sit down in the chair, it's time for some fun!'

Anna Nicod (8)
Feckenham CE First School, Redditch

Football

Manager cross
Manager mad
Corner missed
Corner scored
Boot here
Boot there
Ball up
Ball down
Ball here and there
Ball everywhere
Rude Rooney
Warning Wayne
Massive header
Huge header
Goal scorer
Cross supporters
Mad striker
Goalkeeper.

Alex Oldcorn (8)
Feckenham CE First School, Redditch

Football

Manager, header
Manager, player
Manager, bar
Manager, kick
Manager, corner
Mad-header
Goal saver
Goal rider
Manager, celebrator
Mad goalkeeper
Boot wearer
Ball kicker
Goal scorer
Kit wearer.

Luke Tait (8)
Feckenham CE First School, Redditch

The Teachers

Hand writer
Book marker
Cup of tea maker
Rain hater
Bell ringer
Child moaner
Register ticker
Major worrier
Door shutter
Jewellery lover
Biscuit muncher
Chocolate sneaker
Nail picker
Story reader
Sandwich eater
Summer lover
Winter hater
Educator.

Megan Griffiths (8)
Feckenham CE First School, Redditch

Aliens

My name is Bill and I'm an alien.
I have a brother called Phil.
My brother has another brother and that is me!
I also have a sister who has a giant blister.
I love green and my favourite food is beans.
I'm as green as grass.
My favourite chocolates are Galaxy, Milky Way and Mars bars
Because they're all in space.
I'm Zero the hero and I'm ace.
That's me the *alien!*

Mia Crowe (8)
Feckenham CE First School, Redditch

Aliens

Hello, I'm alien and I'm as green as a bean.
I live on a base in space.
I have a brother and he drives me up the wall.
When I'm feeling mad and a little bit sad,
I make it rain in Spain.
Me, myself, I'm slimy and rhymy.
I have two heads and fifteen eyes,
How about that!
I'm a lot of trouble but I love cuddles.
Now you know my life *is crazy!*

Lucy Gibbs (8)
Feckenham CE First School, Redditch

Doggies

They're tail wagers,
Have cute smiles
Every place they go they bark like they're going crazy
Dogs are curt and the dogs go barking mad and they make me have the worse headache ever.
Good dogs go everywhere like parks, playgrounds and where they want.
Soft as a teddy, as tidy as a bedroom,
As shiny as a rake that shines in the room.

Katie Willis-Ball (8)
Feckenham CE First School, Redditch

Football

Boot wearer
Goal scorer
Goalkeeper
Team player
Bib wearer
Ball dribbler
Skill player
Mad manager.

Alexander Guilfoyle (9)
Feckenham CE First School, Redditch

Space

S tars in space are so surreal, staring at them out of the open window.
P articularly hot all over in the middle and on the outside of it.
A liens are amazing in every single way, living on planets like Mars, Jupiter and Pluto.
C reating new planets every single day, working on them all the time until they are done.
E ating the cheese on the starlit moon in the dark sky of space.

Luke Wade (9)
Feckenham CE First School, Redditch

Roman Soldier

Roman armour
Roman knife
Shielder
Spear user
Sword smasher
Catapulter.

Harry Read (8)
Feckenham CE First School, Redditch

Sea

Crashing waves going in and out of the big bashing rocks.
Very, very cheery jellyfish.
7 or 8 wiggly legs and a bobbed head from an octopus.
A turtle with a shell so colourful and a pattern in each square.
A fish with a black stripe and an orange one.

Olivia Grace Pearce (8)
Feckenham CE First School, Redditch

Roman Soldiers

We like marching, wearing sandals in shiny helmets.
When the battle begins we start to slaughter.
We go to sea and invade the Celts, we have generals.
Every year we live in Roman villas.
We are the strongest empire in the world!

Rhian Tye (8)
Feckenham CE First School, Redditch

The Magic Box
(Based on 'Magic Box' by Kit Wright)

I will put in my box . . .
The tip of a Megladon's fin
And a blue sun
A tiger ready to growl.

I will put in my box . . .
The very first shark stalking in the Pacific Ocean,
The splash of children playing in the swimming pool,
The first kiss of a mum and dad to a child.

I will put in the box . . .
The first knight to have his armour,
The fourth dragon,
A bird singing its tweeting tune.

My box is crafted from the strongest iron, the softest silk
And the stars of space,
With a swooping phoenix on the lid and a girl riding on a noble
Stallion on the corners.
Its hinges are the brothers and sisters holding hands.

I will float in my box,
Through endless dreams
Where superheroes fight dragons
And goblins battle phoenixes
Surrounded by mountainous terrain.

Fred Foley (7)
Holmer Lake Primary School, Telford

Happiness

Happiness is a joy with other people.
Happiness is always when you are with your true love.
Happiness is when you are skipping in the safari park.
Happiness is when you always get together as a family.
Happiness is when you are going on holiday.
Happiness is when you are going on a trip.
Happiness is a long stroll across the beach.
Happiness is always on a sunny day.

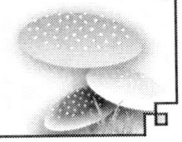

Keavy Evans (10)
Holmer Lake Primary School, Telford

The Magic Box
(Based on 'Magic Box' by Kit Wright)

I will put in my box . . .
Gliding butterflies that fly all day long
A chunk of the hottest sun that is still there in the dark
The first romantic wedding.

I will put in my box . . .
The first smile of a baby
Elephant's tusks that are as a big as a whale
A little girl hugging its pink teddy
And a whale's fin.

I will put in my box . . .
Sparkling fireworks that bang and pop
A horse that gallops to its heart's content
And a romantic kiss from a husband and wife.

My box is created from,
Ice, steel and clear glass
With sparkly sequins on the lid
And ghosts that whisper secrets in the corners.

I shall surf in my box,
On the high waves and the smooth sea
I will surf on the wild Atlantic
Then wash ashore on a yellow beach.

Caitlin Morgan (8)
Holmer Lake Primary School, Telford

Family Pain

This is a poem about family pain.
One thing is also about the rain.
My brother is big and strong, not to mention he pongs.
My sister is a pain in the neck.
My family tree is ginormous.

This is a poem about family pain.
The next part is about the rain.
My niece hates it when it rains.
My mother always has a pain.
I think I need to slouch.

Brandon Rowson-Streames
Holmer Lake Primary School, Telford

Feelings

There are so many different feelings,
Of which I know.
Even if you don't want them,
They will never go.

Anger burns like fire
And is truly a horrible thing,
For if you catch the dreadful disease,
Depression it will bring.

But when that feeling washes away,
Happiness takes its place.
A feeling you want to tie to you
With a giant shoe lace.

Love is an incredible feeling,
Probably the best.
A feeling mixed with happiness,
That certainly beats the rest.

There are many different feelings,
Of which I know,
Even if you don't want them,
They will never go.

Robert Gibbons (10)
Holmer Lake Primary School, Telford

Calm

It is a blue as the sky.
I can smell rice pudding with jam.
Nature is nice and calm to hear.
Birds singing with joy.
I have a minty freshness in my mouth.
A sweetness of jam tarts.
It was so calm.

Matthew Kershaw (9)
Holmer Lake Primary School, Telford

The Magic Box
(Based on 'Magic Box' by Kit Wright)

I will put in my box . . .
Family pictures from a long time ago,
My first disco at school,
A dying grandad's laugh.

I will put in my box . . .
A dragon unfolding its wings,
A newborn kitten,
An unselfish teacher teaching us.

I will put in my box . . .
A kitten opening its eyes on a soft blanket,
My first friends at school,
Casting a birthday wish.

My box is made from spiderwebs and silk
With oak on the lid and waterfalls in the corners.
Its hinges are a killer whale's lips.

I will fly on a magic carpet in my box,
Up to the biggest, huge, gigantic mountain called Snowdon.
Look down anxiously to the bottom,
That has millions of rocks crumbling down.

Karl Kellam (7)
Holmer Lake Primary School, Telford

Love

The colour of pink roses.
Blue dreamy skies above me.
Big cuddles and kisses.
Violets and primroses fill the air.
Birds chirping in the treetop.
That is what I call love, divine.

Tiffany Owen (9)
Holmer Lake Primary School, Telford

The Magic Box
(Based on 'Magic Box' by Kit Wright)

I will put in my box . . .
A sly witch sneaking in people's houses.
A rainbow forming in the sky.
A cat chasing a mouse into people's houses.

I will put in my box . . .
A first born baby,
A boy chasing his escaping kite,
An excited girl chasing a giggling boy.

I will put in my box . . .
A hug from my mom
A first walk from a toddler
A present from Santa Claus.

My box is crafted from stars, diamonds and aluminium,
With a fairy dancing in the sky and shooting stars in the corners.
Its hinges are the jaws of a crocodile.

I will sail in my box,
Up into hot Egypt,
Then look down,
On the people sweating in the sun.

Jeremy Abbey (7)
Holmer Lake Primary School, Telford

Spooked

Spooked is the colour of black.
It smells like dirty socks, misty smoke.
The taste of cold rice pudding makes me shiver.
The floorboards creak beneath my feet.
I feel wet paint that has just been finished.
All of this spooks me!

Daniel Gunnell (10)
Holmer Lake Primary School, Telford

I Have Fun All Day

I'm always having fun,
Every single day,
When I'm with my friends,
We shout hip hip hooray.

I have fun when?
I have fun when?
I have fun when . . .
I'm playing with my friends all day.

When I'm playing games,
All day long.
When my friends come,
They knock and say ding-dong.

I have fun when?
I have fun when?
I have fun when . . .
I'm playing games all day.

When I'm having thrills all day,
Even when I hurt my head.
Making sure I have fun,
Even when I've gone to bed.

Lewis Surgenor (10)
Holmer Lake Primary School, Telford

Relaxed

Relaxed tastes like chocolate melting in your mouth
Or strawberry milkshake with a pink straw.
It smells like lavender or roses.
The air is filled with strawberry smells.
When I'm relaxed, I feel like I'm sitting in a leather chair, with a quilt over me!

Francesca Blair-Haines (9)
Holmer Lake Primary School, Telford

The Magic Box
(Based on 'Magic Box' by Kit Wright)

I will put in the box . . .
A galloping stallion,
A first birthday wish,
The birds softly singing.

I will put in the box . . .
A dragon slowly unfolding its wings,
My first lovely school prom,
An angry frustrated boss shouting at the assistant.

I will put in the box . . .
My loving husband,
An intelligent little girl who wrote this poem,
My heartfelt true love.

My box is fashioned from,
Rubies, shiny pebbles and gold iron steel.

I will glide in my box . . .
Across the softest, cosiest land that does not exist,
Then in my dreams, I will return to my happiest days
Full of giggles, smiles and wishes.

Katelyn Fletcher (7)
Holmer Lake Primary School, Telford

Happiness And Sadness

Happiness can mean joyful, also thrilled,
Happiness is pleased and delighted,
Happiness! Happiness! Happiness!

The opposite of happiness is sadness,
The opposite of sadness is happiness,
Opposite! Opposite! Opposite!

Sadness can mean unhappy, down and low,
Sadness means in the blue and depressed,
Sadness! Sadness! Sadness!

You feel happy at Christmas,
You feel sad when you lose a game,
You feel happy! You feel sad!

Dylan Gillett (10)
Holmer Lake Primary School, Telford

The Magic Box
(Based on 'Magic Box' by Kit Wright)

I will put in my box . . .
Some roses for Mom
A precious ruby-red jewel
A cake for Dad.

I will put in my box . . .
A first rainbow in a blue sky,
My ancient family photos
My family's loving heart.

I will put in my box . . .
A kiss from a newborn baby
Lots of holiday memories
Friends that never forget.

My box is made from glittering, galvanised steel and platinum,
With shooting stars on the lid and children hiding in the corners.
Its hinges are son and loving father holding hands.

I will float in my box
To my dream where knights and dragons fight for victory,
Surrounded by catapults and arrows everywhere.

Ethan Lamb (7)
Holmer Lake Primary School, Telford

My First Love

My first love,
Is my friend,
My first love,
She drives me around the bend.

My first love,
Is so kind,
My first love,
You never know what she might find.

My first love,
Is my friend,
My first love,
Drives me around the bend.

Jack Williams (11)
Holmer Lake Primary School, Telford

Terror

Terror! Terror! everywhere.
Under my bed, in the air,
Scary noises popping out.
They're so creepy, that's no doubt.

Have you ever been alone,
Heard the crunching of a bone?
Terror shrieks, terror cries, terror shouts, terror lies.
One before the Devil said,
'I'm so scared, that's why I'm red.'

People cry when terror comes,
Most call for their mums.
I know the feeling, I really do,
Terror feels like slimy goo!

My friend has a coin that he keeps with him,
It protects him when the sky goes dim.
Terror shrieks, terror cries, terror shouts, terror lies.
Terror!

Alex Clayton (10)
Holmer Lake Primary School, Telford

The Undefeatable War

Bang, bang, what's that sound?
Bang, bang, someone's got a wound
Knock-knock, on the door they reveal the horrifying news,
We hear some people crying,
We hear someone's dying,
You won't believe what we saw,
No more bullets, we're too poor!
Bang, bang, what's that sound?
Thankfully the war will stop very soon,
Bang, bang, Hitler's bombing,
We have no time to be sobbing.
Just run, run, run,
Under the setting sun
Five years after,
We declare peace for ever after,
Finally we get to enjoy laughter!

Joshua Thomas (10)
Holmer Lake Primary School, Telford

The Magic Box
(Based on 'Magic Box' by Kit Wright)

I will put in a box . . .
My first romantic true love,
A first lovely dance with my husband,
A little girl flying her kite that was swooping in the air,
The amazing teacher who feeds me my learning.

I will put in my box . . .
The first smile of a baby,
Elephant's tusks that are as big as a whale,
A little girl hugging its pink teddy.

I will put in my box . . .
A wave splashing at the bumpy and rough shells,
A cowboy galloping on a steel path,
A fancy restaurant selling delicious food.

My box is crafted from gold, silk and paper,
With meadow of flowers on the lid and dancing fairies in the corners.
Its hinges are gold, precious and never to be touched.

Courtney Dean (7)
Holmer Lake Primary School, Telford

I Love My Mum

I love my mum, I really do,
She's everything to me.
My mum's like a bright star,
Twinkling happily.
She turns my frown upside down,
With everything she says.
When I'm ill she's really caring,
And checks on me every now and then.
When she hugs and kisses me,
She makes me feel loved.
When she says she loves me,
I know it's really true.
I love my mum I really do,
She's everything to me.
There's nothing else I can really say,
Apart from I really love you.

Lauryn Proudman (10)
Holmer Lake Primary School, Telford

The Magic Box
(Based on 'Magic Box' by Kit Wright)

I will put in my box . . .
A breath of a dragon
A spark of fire at Bonfire Night.
A scream from a girl being chased by a boy.

I will put in my box . . .
A reaching hand trying to make friends,
A crazy wind whizzing through the sky,
A delicious strawberry chocolate fountain.

My box is made from glass, silk and steel
With twinkling stars on the lid
And sparkling sunlight in the corners.
The hinges are stretchy melted cheese.

I will travel in my box to France
And see how the people live
And see paintings that are famous,
From people long ago.

Kai Mason (8)
Holmer Lake Primary School, Telford

The Magic Box
(Based on 'Magic Box' by Kit Wright)

I will put in my box . . .
A firework shooting in the blue-black sky,
A little baby doing its first steps,
A little newborn baby puppy
A little girl wishing to a dancing fairy,
I will travel in my box . . .
To France and I will fly in my hot air balloon,
Then it will be very hot and red and pink,
It will take me to Paris.
The balloon will take me back home and I will stay there.
I will travel in my box . . .
In my deepest dreams
Then dragons will be breathing fire out of their enormous nostrils.
It will get hurt and run away to its cave.

Anika Francis (7)
Holmer Lake Primary School, Telford

The Magic Box
(Based on 'Magic Box' by Kit Wright)

I put in my box . . .
A newborn dog eating its food
A baby's first cry.

I put in my box . . .
A warm teddy
A silver shooting star.

I will put in my box . . .
A puppy being born
A cat eating its food.

My box is crafted from melting chocolate, stones and shells
With shining berries on the lid and in the corners.
Its hinges are shining rubies.

I will fly in my box up into the soft clouds.
Then look down on the tiny pointed pyramids
That are surrounded by scurrying people that look like little ants.

Bonnie Boylett (7)
Holmer Lake Primary School, Telford

The Egyptian Creation Poem

E gypt was started with a man called Nun, the ruler of everyone.
G loomy seas started to shrivel around
Y ears went by and he still sat lonely with no sound or anything
P eople with no home could not take it anymore.
T ons of rocks scattered around
I t showed up to be an island called Ben-Ben
A tum was the first god and ruled that land
N un did not feel any more loneliness now Atum was here.

C reation of the sun or moon tonight
R a created sun or moon with a stroke of his clock
E nabling sun and the moon to go up
A greeing to a bubble going up to Earth
T ill then Osiris and Iris came over here
I ris saw Seth come over to all of them
O siris died and Seth became ruler
N othing but Osiris under the afterlife to death.

Isha Mal (8)
Holmer Lake Primary School, Telford

Friend

When I read these words today,
They make me think of you
And the memories we share,
That will last a lifetime through.

You are as sweet as honey,
Stacked upon the shelf,
You lay a smile upon my face,
You make the city sunny.

When I was a young girl,
I dreamt of a friend like you.
I think about you all the time,
In everything I do.

I know that our friendship,
Will a long, long time last
And will be cherished just as much,
When today becomes the past.

Abigail Hopley (10)
Holmer Lake Primary School, Telford

The Magic Box
(Based on 'Magic Box' by Kit Wright)

I will put in the box . . .
Cheers from the crowd,
Singing from the supporters,
The kick of a ball.

I will put in the box . . .
A football pen,
A football pad,
I will travel in my box to mountainous, sunny France,
Then look at the people to see how they live.

I will fly in my box,
Up into the soft clouds,
Then look down on the tiny, pointed pyramids,
That are surrounded by scurrying little ants
And dragons floating, stopping bombs on the
End of crossbows, and there are flames coming out of them.

Corey Thomas (8)
Holmer Lake Primary School, Telford

The Happiness

Happiness is love
Happiness is heart
Happiness is soul
Happiness is fun.

I run around on the playground
I run and shout
The wind in my face
I love to be so happy.

Happiness is love
Happiness is heart
Happiness is soul
Happiness is joy and fun.

Happiness is everywhere
Like Mom kisses
On the cheek
Don't be sad, be happy!

Katie Edwards (10)
Holmer Lake Primary School, Telford

The Egyptian Creation Poem

Endless seas everywhere and it was stormy and dark
Great seas rumbled and land appeared
Yellow sand on the hill
Protecting god Atum, protecting the land
Touching the yellow sand on the ground
Itching his back with his hand, wandering around the hill
Atum and Nun were friends
Nun and Atum were happy and pleased, it was a good time.

Creating the God of Air called Shu, protecting Atum with air
Ra created the sun and the rocky moon by sticking it on Nut
Everything was dark and the seas were still there
Atum, Shu, Nut and Ra they created Osisris, Iris and Seth
Telling everyone it was so dark, they were very worried
Iris and Osiris were king and queen of the afterlife
Osiris was pleased but Seth was jealous so he wanted to kill him
Nun was still there but Seth killed Osiris, who went to the afterlife.

Owen Kershaw (8)
Holmer Lake Primary School, Telford

The Egyptian Creation Poem

Egyptian god Nun was lonely and sad as he's never been
God Nun shouted, then the island Ben-Ben resulted
Yellow beams of light appeared on Ben-Ben and
It was the god Atum who protected the island.

Poor Nun was still angry
He needed something that was missing
The island Ben-Ben was hit with gallons of water
It was unbelievable, it was snowing and the gods were confused.

Atum created Nut to protect the air and weather
Nut created the sky to protect the air
Creation of the moon and sun was slowly taking place
Thanks to Nut.

Ra was created to protect the moon and the sun
Everyone wanted to create life
Plants, animals and people
After a while Iris and Osiris were king and queen.

Sean Clancy (9)
Holmer Lake Primary School, Telford

The Egyptian Creation Poem

E gyptian god Nun was created the God of Water.
G od called Atum appeared on a land called Ben-Ben.
Y ears later Atum spat out a god called Shu, the God of Air.
P eople like the gods who made all the land.
T ons of gods were made for all different kinds of things.
I ce was made and everything else.
A tum was the king of all the gods.
N ut was the god of the Sky.

C reation of the world is happiness.
R a created the singing sun and the gloomy moon
E ventually the world happened.
A n amazing person came towards Nun, he was king now
T he sea's waves came to cover
I t was amazing how he created everything
O ne was killed by Seth, who became King of the Afterlife
N ow everything was created.

Ellie Kearney (8)
Holmer Lake Primary School, Telford

The Magic Box
(Based on 'Magic Box' by Kit Wright)

I will put in my box . . .
A well-worn, threadbare teddy.
A leaping frog.
A picture from the past.

I will put in my box . . .
A baby's first word.
A new rainbow.
A friendship bracelet.

My box is created from red roses, fairy dust and pixies' wishes
With fairies dancing on the lid and stars glowing in the corners,
Its hinges are golden, old and rusty.

I will fly in my box up into the soft clouds,
Then look down on the tiny, pointed pyramids
That are surrounded by scurrying little ants.

Meagan Jones (8)
Holmer Lake Primary School, Telford

Relaxed

Relaxed is like the colour of a rose
And it smells like lavender
The taste is like a strawberry that is fresh
It feels like a lovely hot holiday
As I sit down I hear the sound of people in a pool
Relaxed is the best thing to think of.

Ebonie Thomas (10)
Holmer Lake Primary School, Telford

Relaxed!

A beautiful flower with a colourful butterfly fluttering above.
The sweet smell of roses fill the air.
Soft, satin, pink petals fall to the ground.
Relaxed is calm,
Relaxed is me.

Natasha Laine (9)
Holmer Lake Primary School, Telford

Happy

Happy is yellow, like the taste of sweet cherry pie.
It smells like beautiful roses,
And looks like flowers blowing in the gentle breeze
Happy sounds like the wave on the sea gently rolling you.
Happy makes me feel warm like the sunshine on my skin.

Jamie Barnes (11)
Holmer Lake Primary School, Telford

Relaxed

Yellow flowers dance in the air.
A little girl relaxed once more.
As the flowers danced the air whistled as the sun shone.
The girl was awake once more.

Kirsty Webster (10)
Holmer Lake Primary School, Telford

My Best Shoes

My best shoes
Are pink and sparkly
They are new so I wear them a lot
They are my best shoes ever!

My best dress
Is pink, red and has sparkly spots
It is really nice and new so I wear it a lot
It is my best dress ever!

My best skirt
Is pink and sparkly
It is really comfortable and new, I wear it a lot
It is my best skirt ever!

I am a girl,
And I love pink!

Libby Bailey (7)
Little Dewchurch CE Primary School, Hereford

A Poem

I lay down in bed
Thoughts running through my head,
I did not have a clue
Help! What should I do?

I gave out a shout,
'What should it be about?'
I thought about smoking
But no, that was choking.

Mum thought that was funny
So I asked her for some money,
She said I was cheeky
And yet ever so sneaky.

Then I had an idea
That itself deserved a cheer,
It's my imagination
That will be my salvation.

I don't know where I'm going with this
But I know I want to really please Miss,
I may be unsure about the rest
But at least I can say I've done my best.

This poem really has no meaning,
But it's done the job and got you reading,
That really is all I could ask
Phew! At last I've done the task!

Zack Jenkins (10)
Little Dewchurch CE Primary School, Hereford

My Poem

Woof, Woof is my doggy
Because I didn't want a moggy
He is brown and white and sleeps with me at night
He doesn't go for walks
He is cheap to keep
Because he doesn't eat.

Laura Simpkins (7)
Little Dewchurch CE Primary School, Hereford

Revenge!

Along the terrain,
The dusty terrain.
Lay a skeleton,
A haunted skeleton.
He rose from the dust,
As skeletons must.
To look for revenge,
For his life lost.

He looked in the cities
And in the seas.
He went begging on his knees,
For he who killed him.

He saw a figure,
He looked familiar.
It was him!
The one who killed him!

He walked to him slowly,
Bones rattling.
The man saw the skeleton,
He fled.
The skeleton chased him,
He was trapped.
It's time for revenge,
Mwa, ha, ha, ha, ha, ha.

Marcus Bailey (9)
Little Dewchurch CE Primary School, Hereford

Little Black Puppy

A little black puppy all dark and alone.
A little black puppy trying to find a home.
The little black puppy went to the park
He gave a little bark.
A young man came and picked up the puppy
And they lived together and were very happy.

Jayden Dare (9)
Little Dewchurch CE Primary School, Hereford

Day At The Fair

I went to the fair,
Lots of people were there.
I got a call from my boss,
'Get me some candyfloss,'
I went to a man,
In a big white van.
I gave him some money,
He looked at me funny.
I gave him a frown,
As my face as a clown.
I got on the bumper car,
I didn't go very far.
I went on the ghost train,
Because it started to rain.
It stopped,
Off I hopped.
I hooked a duck,
Just by luck.
So I won a cow
I don't know how.
It was nearly the end,
So I met my friends.

Amie Jenkins (8)
Little Dewchurch CE Primary School, Hereford

Football

Football is the best,
It beats all the rest.

Kicking the ball,
It is so cool.

Sir Alex Ferguson likes his honey,
But professionals have lots of money.

I play for Ross,
My dad is the boss.

When we lose,
We don't drink lots of booze.

Edward Charles (10)
Little Dewchurch CE Primary School, Hereford

My Garden

When all is quiet and dark
My little dog starts to bark
That's the sign they have come
To eat my food and fill their tum
Mr and Mrs Prickles visit every night
Because my garden's a hedgehog's delight
It's full of fruit and nuts and slugs
And tasty things like big fat bugs
Under a hedge sits a cat
Waiting to jump up and catch a bat
And now here comes a rat
Followed by his friends for a chat
What a busy garden it is at night
You better watch out or you'll have a fright.

Esme Lang (7)
Little Dewchurch CE Primary School, Hereford

Mutant Animal

I was rowing on the river in my boat the other day,
When I saw something scary going the other way,
It was its tail that caught my eye,
As it swished elegantly in the water,
And I wish I had my camera because I'd be just like a reporter.
It swam up to the boat, put its beak upon the side,
The look of shock and horror I surely couldn't hide,
It was then that I noticed, it was as scaly as a snake and as slimy as a snail,
At the same time it gave a little wail.
Its eyes as black as coal,
Its tail as long as a pole.
It jumped onto the boat and drenched me completely,
So I jumped off the boat and swam away quickly.

Benjamin Tate (8)
Little Dewchurch CE Primary School, Hereford

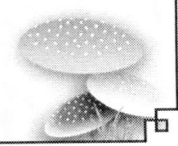

Toffee

Horses are the best, they beat all the rest
My favourite one is Toffee when his ears go all floppy
He loves to eat carrots
But he's not a parrot
He has strong legs
But not in bed
When I trot
I get really hot
When I went on a hack
I think I hurt his back
When I groom his mane it's really soft
Which flies up and makes me cough
I love him with all my heart
I hope we will never part.

Bethany Aldsworth (10)
Little Dewchurch CE Primary School, Hereford

Night Sky Cake

Pinky orange stripes streak
Across the blackening blue sunset bleak,
I turn around and I see
In front of me a gloomy orange lake.

The shape of the lake was like a cake
I saw my mother make
She put the cake in the oven to bake,
After a while I said, 'When's it going to be ready for goodness sake?'

I tried to make shapes out of the colours I saw
I shook and I shook to make the right shape.
I walked across the road
To the lake to see it closer
Then I saw a poster, it was for a piece of chocolate cake.

Melissa Louise Peters (8)
Little Dewchurch CE Primary School, Hereford

Trick Or Treat?

Horrible haunted houses,
Extra loud screams,
Big scary black bats hanging from the beams.

Wonky old trees,
Blowing wildly in the breeze,
Cold white ghosts shivering, knocking their knees.

Trick or treating,
From door to door,
Not enough sweets,
I need more!

Lauren Legge (8)
Little Dewchurch CE Primary School, Hereford

Gunfire

As the guns are shot
Barrels smoking hot,
Why do we fight all through the night
People die
Why, why, why?
This war must end
Or more death is around the bend.

They taste fresh blood in their mouths
As they say their silent vows,
Of returning safe and sound.

Nick Peters (10)
Little Dewchurch CE Primary School, Hereford

He Is A Brilliant Friend

He is brilliant at maths
He is great at acting
He is excellent at singing
He is wonderful at swimming
He is awesome at poetry
He is awesome at Lego
He is brilliant at sleeping
He is always the top of the class
He is excellent at dancing
He is brilliant at friendship.

Susan Hawker (8)
Little Dewchurch CE Primary School, Hereford

The Gnu Who Said Wahoo

There once was a blue gnu
He had lots of shoes
Reds and blues
But he didn't know what to do!

He put on four shoes
Half-red, half-blue
That is two + two
Said the clever blue gnu
Wahoo!

Ellis Shepherd (7)
Little Dewchurch CE Primary School, Hereford

Love

Love can be red,
Love can be blue,
Whenever I'm with you, I never want to go to bed,
Otherwise I'll miss you!
Love can be brown,
Love can be pink,
I wonder what else love can be . . .
I'll think.

Calista Turnell (11)
Loatlands Primary School, Kettering

A Poem About Sheep!

Fluffy as a soft blanket,
As cute as a button.
No one's as cute as a lamb with a big ball of cotton.
Woollen threads of cosy winter wear,
His eyes twinkling throughout the moonlight,
But they leave him out there overnight.
People say that he may bite,
But he thinks to himself, *how I can give them a scary fright?*
Today it's a bright day, I might run out and about,
Sniff, sniff, sniffing with my snout.
Beyond and about, day in, day out,
People can still see my big brown, smelly snout.

Rebecca Lindy Ainsworth
Loatlands Primary School, Kettering

The Midnight Sky

Midnight is the only time to look at the stars alone,
While sitting on a deckchair eating an ice cream cone.
On a full moon people say that ghosts and werewolves come out,
But they are wrong because they are not out and about.
Shining, shiny stars up above,
People may even fall in love!

Hattie Rose Street (10)
Loatlands Primary School, Kettering

Yummy, Yummy Fruit And Veg

Cauliflower furry,
Apples are ripe,
Very yummy in my tummy,
Carrots crunchy, pepper sweet,
These are the veg I like to eat
Harvest is a time to share
Lovely fruit and veg to eat, all to myself, yum-yum!
It's time to plant the seeds
Grow, grow, grow, high, high, high,
Time to take out veg from the ground!

Jaime Anderson (9)
Marlbrook Primary School, Hereford

Harvest Time Is . . .

H arvest smells in the air.
A pples, pears and bananas too.
R ipe and ready to eat.
V egetables are healthy.
E at them.
S mell the fruit and vegetables.
T ouch them all.

T aste them.
I t's a very special time.
M ix lots of vegetables.
E veryone can celebrate by getting together in church.

I love harvest.
S oil is good, it makes things grow.

I like to eat fruit.
M ostly piled.
P otatoes are yummy.
O ranges are too.
R eady to eat.
T ake time to eat them.
A pples are red.
N ice and tasty
T angerines are oranges.

Daisy Morris (9)
Marlbrook Primary School, Hereford

Harvest Poem

Harvest is here,
Time to eat,
Lovely veg we grow,
Don't forget the crops,
Carrots, apples, bananas, are all harvest food,
Eat your veg and fruit.
Share all the time,
Super vegetables,
Don't forget the fruit,
Potatoes don't count as your five-a-day,
Always running about to get your fruit and veg!

Benjamin Nelder (9)
Marlbrook Primary School, Hereford

Celebrate Harvest

Strawberries, carrots,
Potatoes, pears
All foods that we can share
Food that we can eat
Food that we can plant
All food that we can share
Over to the farms to pick the plants
Share it all
Who has none?
Strawberries red
Potatoes brown, growing day and night in the ground
Carrots orange, apples pink,
Ready to be picked
Let's celebrate, harvest it's fun.
Yum! Yum! Yum!

Alexis Foster (9)
Marlbrook Primary School, Hereford

Fruit And Veg Poem

Cauliflower fluffy,
Strawberries sweet,
Broad beans flat,
Peppers green,
Apples green,
Carrots orange,
Beetroot purple,
Potatoes brown,
Bananas yellow,
Blueberries blue,
Plums orangey red,
Seeds different colours,
Tomatoes red.

Loren Prothero (9)
Marlbrook Primary School, Hereford

Maddie's Workshop

Featured Author:

Maddie Stewart

Maddie is a children's writer, poet and author who currently lives in Coney Island, Northern Ireland.

Maddie has 5 published children's books, 'Cinders', 'Hal's Sleepover', 'Bertie Rooster', 'Peg' and 'Clever Daddy'. Maddie uses her own unpublished work to provide entertaining, interactive poems and rhyming stories for use in her workshops with children when she visits schools, libraries, arts centres and book festivals. Favourites are 'Silly Billy, Auntie Millie' and 'I'm a Cool, Cool Kid'. Maddie works throughout Ireland from her home in County Down. She is also happy to work from a variety of bases in England. She has friends and family, with whom she regularly stays, in Leicester, Bedford, London and Ashford (Kent). Maddie's workshops are aimed at 5-11-year-olds. Check out Maddie's website for all her latest news and free poetry resources **www.maddiestewart.com**.

Read on to pick up some fab writing tips!

Nonsense Workshop

If you find silliness fun, you will love nonsense poems. Nonsense poems might describe silly things, or people, or situations, or, any combination of the three.

For example:

When I got out of bed today,
both my arms had run away.
I sent my feet to fetch them back.
When they came back, toe in hand
I realised what they had planned.
They'd made the breakfast I love most,
buttered spider's eggs on toast.

One way to find out if you enjoy nonsense poems is to start with familiar nursery rhymes. Ask your teacher to read them out, putting in the names of some children in your class.

Like this: Troy and Jill went up the hill
to fetch a pail of water.
Troy fell down
and broke his crown
and Jill came tumbling after.

If anyone is upset at the idea of using their name, then don't use it.

Did you find this fun?

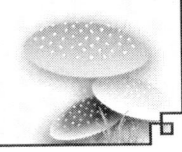

Maddie's Workshop

**Now try changing a nursery rhyme.
Keep the rhythm and the rhyme style, but invent a silly situation.**

Like this: Hickory Dickory Dare
a pig flew up in the air.
The clouds above
gave him a shove
Hickory Dickory Dare.

Or this: Little Miss Mabel
sat at her table
eating a strawberry pie
but a big, hairy beast
stole her strawberry feast
and made poor little Mabel cry.

How does your rhyme sound if you put your own name in it?

**Another idea for nonsense poems is to pretend letters are people
and have them do silly things.**

For example:
| Mrs A | Mrs B | Mrs C |
| Lost her way | Dropped a pea | Ate a tree |

**To make your own 'Silly People Poem', think of a word to use.
To show you an example, I will choose the word 'silly'.
Write your word vertically down the left hand side of your page.
Then write down some words which rhyme
with the sound of each letter.**

S mess, dress, Bess, chess, cress
I eye, bye, sky, guy, pie, sky
L sell, bell, shell, tell, swell, well
L " " " " " " (" means the same as written above)
Y (the same words as those rhyming with I)

Use your rhyming word lists to help you make up your poem.

Mrs S made a mess
Mrs I ate a pie
Mrs L rang a bell
Mrs L broke a shell
Mrs Y said 'Bye-bye.'

You might even make a 'Silly Alphabet' by using all the letters of the alphabet.

It is hard to find rhyming words for all the letters. H, X and W are letters which are hard to match with rhyming words. I'll give you some I've thought of:

H - cage, stage, wage (close but not perfect)
X - flex, specs, complex, Middlesex
W - trouble you, chicken coop, bubble zoo

However, with nonsense poems, you can use nonsense words. You can make up your own words.

To start making up nonsense words you could try mixing dictionary words together. Let's make up some nonsense animals.

Make two lists of animals. (You can include birds and fish as well.)

Your lists can be as long as you like. These are lists I made:

elephant	kangaroo
tiger	penguin
lizard	octopus
monkey	chicken

Now use the start of an animal on one list and substitute it for the start of an animal from your other list.

I might use the start of oct/opus ... oct and substitute it for the end of l/izard to give me a new nonsense animal ... an octizard.
I might swap the start of monk/ey ... monk with the end of kang/aroo To give me another new nonsense animal ... a monkaroo.

What might a monkaroo look like? What might it eat?

You could try mixing some food words in the same way, to make up nonsense foods.

cabbage	potatoes
lettuce	parsley
bacon	crisps

Cribbage, bacley, and lettatoes are some nonsense foods made up from my lists.

Let's see if I can make a nonsense poem about my monkaroo.

Maddie's Workshop

My monkaroo loves bacley.
He'll eat lettatoes too
But his favourite food is cribbage
Especially if it's blue.

Would you like to try and make up your own nonsense poem?

**Nonsense words don't have to be a combination of dictionary words.
They can be completely 'made up'.
You can use nonsense words to write nonsense sonnets,
or list poems or any type of poem you like.**

Here is a poem full of nonsense words:

I melly micked a turdle
and flecked a pendril's tum.
I plotineyed a shugat
and dracked a pipin's plum.

**Ask your teacher to read it putting in some children's names instead
of the first I, and he or she instead of the second I.**

Did that sound funny?

You might think that nonsense poems are just silly and not for the serious poet.
However poets tend to love language. Making up your own words is a natural
part of enjoying words and sounds and how they fit together. Many poets love the
freedom nonsense poems give them. Lots and lots of very famous poets have written
nonsense poems. I'll name some: **Edward Lear**, **Roger McGough**, **Lewis Carroll**,
Jack Prelutsky and **Nick Toczek**. Can you or your teacher think of any more?
For help with a class nonsense poem or to find more nonsense nursery rhymes look
on my website, **www.maddiestewart.com**. Have fun! Maddie Stewart.

POETRY TECHNIQUES

HERE IS a SELECTION OF POETRY TECHNIQUES WITH EXAMPLES

Metaphors & Similes

A *metaphor* is when you describe your subject *as* something else, for example: 'Winter is a cruel master leaving the servants in a bleak wilderness' whereas a *simile* describes your subject *like* something else i.e. 'His blue eyes are like ice-cold puddles' or 'The flames flickered like eyelashes'.

Personification

This is to simply give a personality to something that is not human, for example 'Fear spreads her uneasiness around' or 'Summer casts down her warm sunrays'.

Imagery

To use words to create mental pictures of what you are trying to convey, your poem should awaken the senses and make the reader feel like they are in that poetic scene ...
'The sky was streaked with pink and red as shadows cast across the once-golden sand'.
'The sea gently lapped the shore as the palm trees rustled softly in the evening breeze'.

Assonance & Alliteration

Alliteration uses a repeated constant sound and this effect can be quite striking: 'Smash, slippery snake slithered sideways'.
Assonance repeats a significant vowel or vowel sound to create an impact: 'The pool looked cool'.

Repetition

By repeating a significant word the echo effect can be a very powerful way of enhancing an emotion or point your poem is putting across.
'The blows rained down, down,
Never ceasing,
Never caring
About the pain,
The pain'.

Onomatopoeia

This simply means you use words that sound like the noise you are describing, for example 'The rain *pattered* on the window' or 'The tin can *clattered* up the alley'.

Rhythm & Metre

The *rhythm* of a poem means 'the beat', the sense of movement you create. The placing of punctuation and the use of syllables affect the *rhythm* of the poem. If your intention is to have your poem read slowly, use double, triple or larger syllables and punctuate more often, where as if you want to have a fast-paced read use single syllables, less punctuation and shorter sentences.
If you have a regular rhythm throughout your poem this is known as *metre*.

Enjambment

This means you don't use punctuation at the end of your line, you simply let the line flow on to the next one. It is commonly used and is a good word to drop into your homework!

Tone & Lyric

The poet's intention is expressed through their *tone*. You may feel happiness, anger, confusion, loathing or admiration for your poetic subject. Are you criticising or praising? How you feel about your topic will affect your choice of words and therefore your *tone*. For example 'I *loved* her', 'I *cared* for her', 'I *liked* her'.
If you write the poem from a personal view or experience this is referred to as a *lyrical* poem. A good example of a lyrical poem is Seamus Heaney's 'Mid-term Break' or any sonnet!

All About Shakespeare

Try this fun quiz with your family, friends or even in class!

1. Where was Shakespeare born?

....

2. Mercutio is a character in which Shakepeare play?

....

3. Which monarch was said to be 'quite a fan' of his work?

....

4. How old was he when he married?

....

5. What is the name of the last and 'only original' play he wrote?

....

6. What are the names of King Lear's three daughters?

....

7. Who is Anne Hathaway?

....

All About Shakespeare

8. Which city is the play 'Othello' set in?

....

9. Can you name 2 of Shakespeare's 17 comedies?

....

10. 'This day is call'd the feast of Crispian: He that outlives this day, and comes safe home, Will stand a tip-toe when this day is nam'd, and rouse him at the name of Crispian' is a quote from which play?

....

11. Leonardo DiCaprio played Romeo in the modern day film version of Romeo and Juliet. Who played Juliet in the movie?

....

12. Three witches famously appear in which play?

....

13. Which famous Shakespearean character is Eric in the image to the left?

....

14. What was Shakespeare's favourite poetic form?

....

Answers are printed on the last page of the book, good luck!

If you would rather try the quiz online,
you can do so at www.youngwriters.co.uk.

Poetry Activity

Word Soup

**To help you write a poem, or even a story,
on any theme, you should create word soup!**

If you have a theme or subject for your poem, base your word soup on it.
If not, don't worry, the word soup will help you find a theme.

To start your word soup you need ingredients:

- Nouns (names of people, places, objects, feelings, i.e. Mum, Paris, house, anger)
- Colours
- Verbs ('doing words', i.e. kicking, laughing, running, falling, smiling)
- Adjectives (words that describe nouns, i.e. tall, hairy, hollow, smelly, angelic)

We suggest at least 5 of each from the above list, this will make sure your word soup has plenty of choice. Now, if you have already been given a theme or title for your poem, base your ingredients on this. If you have no idea what to write about, write down whatever you like, or ask a teacher or family member to give you a theme to write about.

Poetry Activity

Making Word Soup

Next, you'll need a sheet of paper.
Cut it into at least 20 pieces. Make sure the pieces are big enough to write your ingredients on, one ingredient on each piece of paper.
Write your ingredients on the pieces of paper.
Shuffle the pieces of paper and put them all in a box or bowl
- something you can pick the paper out of without looking at the words.
Pick out 5 words to start and use them to write your poem!

Example:

Our theme is winter. Our ingredients are:
- Nouns: snowflake, Santa, hat, Christmas, snowman.
- Colours: blue, white, green, orange, red.
- Verbs: ice-skating, playing, laughing, smiling, wrapping.
- Adjectives: cold, tall, fast, crunchy, sparkly.

Our word soup gave us these 5 words:
snowman, red, cold, hat, fast and our poem goes like this:

It's a *cold* winter's day,
My nose and cheeks are *red*
As I'm outside, building my *snowman*,
I add a *hat* and a carrot nose to finish,
I hope he doesn't melt too *fast*!

Tip: add more ingredients to your word soup
and see how many different poems you can write!

Tip: if you're finding it hard to write a poem with
the words you've picked, swap a word with another one!

Tip: try adding poem styles and techniques,
such as assonance or haiku to your soup for an added challenge!

SCRIBBLER!

*If you enjoy creative writing then you'll love our magazine, Scribbler!, the fun and educational magazine for 7-11-year-olds that works alongside Key Stage 2 National Literacy Strategy Learning Objectives. For further information visit **www.youngwriters.co.uk**.*

Grammar Fun
Our resident dinosaur Bernard helps to improve writing skills from punctuation to spelling.

Nessie's Workshop
Each issue Nessie explains a style of writing and sets an exercise for you to do. Previous workshops include the limerick, haiku and shape poems.

Awesome Author
Read all about past and present authors. Previous Awesome Authors include Roald Dahl, William Shakespeare and Ricky Gervais!

Once Upon a Time ...
Lord Oscar starts a story ... it's your job to finish it. Our favourite wins a writing set.

Guest Author
A famous author drops by and answers some of our in-depth questions, while donating a great prize to give away. Recent authors include former Children's Laureate Michael Morpurgo, adventurer Bear Grylls and Nick Ward, author of the Charlie Small Journals.

Art Gallery
Send Bizzy your paintings and drawings and his favourite wins an art set including some fab Staedtler goodies.

Puzzle Time!
Could you find Eric? Unscramble Anna Gram's words? Tackle our hard puzzles? If so, winners receive fab prizes.

The Brainiacs
Scribbler!'s own gang of wiz kids are always on hand to help with spellings, alternative words and writing styles, they'll get you on the right track!

Prizes
Every issue we give away fantastic prizes. Recent prizes include Staedtler goodies, signed copies of Bear Grylls' books and posters, signed copies of Ricky Gervais' books, Charlie Small goodie bags, family tickets to The Eden Project, The Roald Dahl Museum & Story Centre and Alton Towers, a digital camera, books and writing sets galore and many other fab prizes!

... plus much more!
We keep you up to date with all the happenings in the world of literature, including blog updates from the Children's Laureate.

*If you are too old for Scribbler! magazine or have an older friend who enjoys creative writing, then check out Wordsmith. Wordsmith is for 11-18-year-olds and is jam-packed full of brilliant features, young writers' work, competitions and interviews too. For further information check out **www.youngwriters.co.uk** or ask an adult to call us on (01733) 890066.*

To get an adult to subscribe to either magazine for you, ask them to visit the website or give us a call.

It's Autumn

A little girl is wearing autumn,
Colourful tights,
Red knitted gloves,
Cosy and warm.
Brown dull hat,
It's really cold,
Black woollen scarf around her neck,
A dark purple coat,
With her belt tied around her waist.
Bright yellow skirt,
And she loves the breakable leaves which turn
Red and golden orange.
And a really warm T-shirt.

Jasmine Edkins (10)
Marlbrook Primary School, Hereford

Autumn

He takes off his brown leather jacket,
While looking for yellow leaves.
He strips off his old clothes
And straps on his new warm clothes.
He wears his brown, soft gloves,
A yellow woolly hat
And a ginger scarf,
When he walks out of the door,
All of a sudden, it is quiet,
Then different coloured leaves
All fly into the air.
The trees are whistling,
It's autumn.

James Venables (10)
Marlbrook Primary School, Hereford

Food Glorious Food

Food glorious food
Strawberries and apples
They are all harvest things
That we can eat
Delicious yummy treats
Very nice indeed
Juicy, ripe and red
Bananas smooth and yellow
Best I've ever seen
Carrots crunchy
Beetroot sweet
That's what people like to eat.

Mia Rumsey (9)
Marlbrook Primary School, Hereford

It's Autumn

When he comes
Dark mornings arise.
Razor-sharp conkers fall.
The golden leaves fall.
Trees whistle in the wind
A brave, strong, muscular, white tiger creeps,
Like a cold day when it snows.
The joyful wind swirls, twirls, whirls around,
Picking up a pile of leaves
And tossing them around.
Leaves changing colour,
Like a white tiger bolting through mud.

Tyler Chatterley-Russell (10)
Marlbrook Primary School, Hereford

A Hippo

A hippo has got a big back,
A hippo has got a fat belly,
A hippo has sharp teeth and a little tail,
A hippo has a bath in the lake.

Spencer Young (7)
Marlbrook Primary School, Hereford

Harvest Poem

Harvest is time for sharing food,
It puts me in a happy mood.
The apples are smooth and the berries are sour,
If you eat them all it will give you special power.
I can hear the birdies tweet,
The sound is so, so sweet.
The crops in the ground are growing fast,
The veg gets bigger as the time goes past.
The pears on the trees are ready to fall,
Yum-yum we can eat them all.
Harvest has come to an end
So be grateful you've got all this my friend.

Lauren Perkins (9)
Marlbrook Primary School, Hereford

It's Autumn

Autumn is cold all around.
Snails curl into their little shells.
Autumn feels like the cold wind flowing past you.
Autumn tastes like cold food.
Butterflies go away on holiday.
Autumn looks like the brown leaves falling off the trees.
Autumn is the cold rain.
Autumn is a big brown pile of leaves.
Autumn is a dark morning.
Autumn is when we do not go on holiday.
Autumn is when slimy mud is on the ground.

Curtis Jenkins (11)
Marlbrook Primary School, Hereford

Autumn

The beautiful brown mare of autumn
Gingery orange
Galloping happily
Through the peaceful orchards
Enjoying the cold breeze.

Rachelle Jaine Barrall (10)
Marlbrook Primary School, Hereford

Harvest

H arvest is a time where we love and share.
A nniversary, Christmas, nothing like this.
R aising the food from the deep dark soil.
V ast potatoes and sweet grapes.
E ating and sharing that's all we ask.
S hare, that's all it's about.
T hank you for listening and happy harvest!

Happy harvest.

Alexander Baker (9)
Marlbrook Primary School, Hereford

Harvest

Harvest is a time where we don't have to wait
For the lovely food to grow
For when we harvest
We share it with love
Red strawberries redder than ever
Orange carrots, orange as the sun
Brown potatoes straight from the mud
Green apples, green as the grass.

Callum Harding (9)
Marlbrook Primary School, Hereford

Harvest

H arvest is a great time to share.
A pples, potatoes and carrots.
R ainfall is to make the vegetables.
V egetables - it's a good time to eat them.
E veryone say thank you for all the wonderful food we have just eaten and
   set sail to their country.
S ow the seeds in the land.
T rees are where vegetables grow.

Marshall Turner (9)
Marlbrook Primary School, Hereford

Monkeys

Monkeys are greedy,
They like bananas,
Monkeys are furry and brown,
Monkeys live in a jungle,
Which is usually very wet.
Monkeys swing from tree to tree and vine to vine.
Monkeys have small mouths,
Very sharp teeth, really.

Lucy Silver (7)
Marlbrook Primary School, Hereford

It's Autumn

A visit to the salon
To change her hair colour,
From luminous green
To chocolate-brown.
A blast of cold air
Moulding into icy peaks
She aborts her summer clothes
Replacing them with thicker, warmer attire.

Keaton Glancy (10)
Marlbrook Primary School, Hereford

It's Autumn

She goes to the salon
To change her hair colour
To golden yellow, ruby red and chocolate brown.
She takes off her gruesome green coat
And puts on her beautiful brown one.
Then she gently whirls home
And cries so much with gigantic tears,
I'm autumn!

Dominica Allfrey (10)
Marlbrook Primary School, Hereford

Monkeys

Monkeys have a big curly tail, like little spirals,
Monkeys have a very funny brown face,
Monkeys have paws like cats and dogs,
Monkeys have sharp claws like tigers and lions.

Monkeys have strong legs so they can walk, climb or run quickly,
Monkeys have big ears with little curls,
Monkeys have fruit and bananas for lunch, dinner and tea.

Candice Hooper (7)
Marlbrook Primary School, Hereford

Celebrate Harvest

Harvest is a happy time,
When all the seeds have grown.
Children munching on all the fruit and veg,
Which are sweet strawberries and crunchy carrots
And so much more
Children tasting the ripe apples and all other fruit and veg,
While hearing the crows tweeting above their heads.

Ashleigh Jenkins (9)
Marlbrook Primary School, Hereford

Let's Celebrate Harvest

H arvest is the time we share gifts,
A pples are sweet and bananas are yellow.
R ipe in the ground are potatoes,
V ery yummy.
E ating it all up yummy, yummy,
S itting down and enjoying and having fun.
T hen harvest has finished yum, yum, yum.

Lauren Francis (9)
Marlbrook Primary School, Hereford

Harvest

Fruit and vegetables.
The best of the best.
That is what we eat.
Grown with pride.
And many hands.
Fruit and vegetables
Grow on these fine lands.

Chloe Grant (9)
Marlbrook Primary School, Hereford

Untitled

Harvest time is here,
Lots of lovely food to eat.
Lots of soil on the ground.
Veg in the ground waiting to grow!
Carrots so crunchy,
Brown potatoes soft as a fluffy feather.
Apples ripening in the sun.

Dylan Jones (9)
Marlbrook Primary School, Hereford

Harvest

Harvest, harvest, where's the fruit?
Harvest, harvest let's celebrate
Harvest, harvest, everybody eat
Harvest, harvest, eat, eat, eat.
Everybody farmer's coming
Jump, jump, jump for joy,
Harvest, harvest, it's coming now.

Chloe Pegrum (9)
Marlbrook Primary School, Hereford

A Bird

A bird can fly,
A bird can sing.
It can fly from tree to tree.
A bird hatches from eggs.
A bird lives in a nest.
It catches worms for its tea.

Bethany Mason (7)
Marlbrook Primary School, Hereford

Harvest Fruit And Veg

Harvest is a time to show that we care,
To dig the hole in the soil,
To share the carrots, the peas and not forgetting the apples,
To share at the harvest, harvest we love the veg,
All the food is yummy to eat,
Fruit is good for your teeth.

Imogen Lavell (9)
Marlbrook Primary School, Hereford

It's Autumn

He slowly saunters through the leaves
Floating down steadily all around him
Bravely, he twists and changes the season
He strides, trots carelessly through the street
Feeling the dampness of the special rain.

Abbie Crawford (10)
Marlbrook Primary School, Hereford

It's Autumn

She charges proudly through the dark night
Dressed in her furry brown overcoat,
Putting on her fluffy yellow boots
Over her warm purple leggings.
Gone are her summer clothes.

Caitlin Bethell (10)
Marlbrook Primary School, Hereford

Autumn

Autumn turns off her torch making darker mornings.
She strips off her old clothes
And puts on her brown rustic fleece.
Autumn puts on her white coat,
Making colder mornings.

James Oakley (10)
Marlbrook Primary School, Hereford

Dream Bottle Poem

In the book jar is a leaf from the tallest tree,
Is a drop from the saltiest sea,
Is a rare flower from a mythical land,
Is not a drop of red at all.

Saffron Scott (8)
Marlbrook Primary School, Hereford

A Dolphin

A dolphin is blue or grey,
A dolphin has a smooth back,
A dolphin has sharp teeth,
Dolphins are pink when they are babies.

Emilie May Preedy (7)
Marlbrook Primary School, Hereford

Dogs

Dogs are cute,
Cuddly and smart,
They capture your heart.
When in need of attention
They start to bark.
They melt your heart
When they whimper.
My dog, Freddie, is a friendly soul
But sometimes he gets out of control!

Charlotte Hughes (8)
Norbury Primary School, Bishops Castle

What Am I?

A high jumper,
A fast runner,
A strong swimmer,
A dog biter.

A water shaker,
A fun player,
A sad howler,
A naughty toddler.

A puddle piddler,
A sneaky stealer,
An inquisitive sniffer,
An everyday eater.

A patient listener,
A good thinker.

What am I?
A: A dog

Braden Colley (8)
Norbury Primary School, Bishops Castle

My Dogs

Crazy,
Funny,
Pretty,
Sly,
Silly,
Naughty,
Full of love,
Black and white,
Eyes glinting in the sun,
Bird catchers,
Food gulpers,
Best to make me happy,
Best friends.
My dogs,
Pip and Meg!

Charlotte Muller (10)
Norbury Primary School, Bishops Castle

What Am I?

A runner
A fidgeter
A loud purrer
A back scratcher
A black spotter
A lazy snorer
A true lover
A big hunter
A fast eater
A cruncher
A big clawer
What am I?
A: A cat

Anni Lloyd-Langford (7)
Norbury Primary School, Bishops Castle

Thomas, The Cat

Thomas is a cat.
A very friendly cat.
A very hungry cat.
Wise green eyes focusing on his food.
Thomas is a cat.
A very funny cat.
A very playful cat.
Wise green eyes focusing on his toy.
Thomas is a cat.
A very sleepy cat.
A very tired cat.
Wise green eyes . . . shut.

Jake Varcoe (10)
Norbury Primary School, Bishops Castle

Trinity

Trinity is funny,
She always says stuff is yummy,
Trinity is cute and nice,
She gives very good advice,
She's a great tickler,
She loves the name Nicola,
She likes playing with dolls,
She likes digging holes,
She likes going to the zoo to play peekaboo!
Trinity has blonde hair,
She sits on a chair.

Grace Davies (7)
Norbury Primary School, Bishops Castle

What Is It?

It's green
It's brown
It's black
It's dead
In a sleepy bed
It's dirty
It's angry
It's sad
Because one hundred are dead.
What is it?
A: A soldier.

Rohan Colley (8)
Norbury Primary School, Bishops Castle

Autumn Witches

Leafy autumn witches cackle under feet,
Sending gales of magic through the burning trees,
They set the trees up in flames of orange, yellow and red,
The brown cinders spin slowly to the soily ground,
They strip the trees with frosty hands,
Shrieking and shouting till the frost queen lifts her veil.

Jodie Betton (10)
Norbury Primary School, Bishops Castle

Things I Have Been Doing Lately

Playing on Jodie's DS
Fiddling with my hair
Playing with my friend
Nagging my mum and dad
Calling Jodie 'it'
Tapping my pencil on me
Rocking on my chair
Playing games
Sucking my thumb
Biting my nails
Having fun!

Kirsty Betton (8)
Norbury Primary School, Bishops Castle

My Friends

Pizza lovers
Secret hiders
Smile makers
Basketball players
Pet lovers
Loud screamers
Chocolate munchers
Friendship keepers
It's my friends all over!

Amelia Jones (10)
Norbury Primary School, Bishops Castle

Sorol

Sorol is the best guinea pig we've had!
He's white and ginger all over,
He doesn't like Dad!
He's ecstatic and lively.
He never wants to stop!
He loves . . . jumping, running, hopping,
Sorol loves us.
We've nearly had him six months!

Sophie Gillin (10)
Norbury Primary School, Bishops Castle

What To Do

'Mum, can I teach Buzby how to buck?'
'No!'
'Mum can I teach Buzby how to jump on you?'
'No!'
'Mum can I teach Buzby how to get out of the field and eat your flowers?'
'No!'
'Mum can I teach Buzby to open doors?'
'Fine, but be careful.'

Rebecca Speich (7)
Norbury Primary School, Bishops Castle

Wayne Rooney

There is a player for Man Utd
Who gets all the goals.
He always get the ball in the hole.
He's the star of the lot.
His football skills are so hot.
I am talking about Wayne Rooney.

Louis Wood (10)
Norbury Primary School, Bishops Castle

Bunny

I had a bunny
Who stole my money,
It wasn't funny,
He brought some honey,
He was yummy,
In my tummy.

Millie Wood (8)
Norbury Primary School, Bishops Castle

My Favourite Pig

When I see you, you grunt a little song
When I go outside I smell a big pong
If I didn't see you my life wouldn't be complete
You're a pretty diamond
You're the best pig!

Olivia Littlehales (8)
Norbury Primary School, Bishops Castle

Dunkan

When I see Duncan
He always gives me a wave
When he is drumming
He always plays loud
He is always excellent.

Milo Turner (7)
Norbury Primary School, Bishops Castle

Sorel, The Dog

She is big, brave and never misbehaves,
She's always there on Monday days.
She barks at cars day and night,
Sorel, I love her with all my might.

Lola McCormack (9)
Norbury Primary School, Bishops Castle

Rocky

Rocky, Rocky is so stocky.
He likes to play horsey hockey.
Rocky, Rocky is so stocky.
He likes to play with his friend Donkey Dive.

Sally Watney (7)
Norbury Primary School, Bishops Castle

My Car

My car has power
It goes 50 miles per hour
It is big, it goes slow
But I like my car.

Tom Jarratt (7)
Norbury Primary School, Bishops Castle

Lifeguard

Life saver,
First aider,
Flip-flop wearer,
Emergency helper,
Child watcher,
Confident person,
Fast swimmer,
Amazing diver,
What am I?
A: A lifeguard.

Annabel Holt (10)
Perrywood Primary & Nursery School, Worcester

Doctor

People talker,
Disease curer,
Medicine giver,
Life saver,
Illness helper,
Hard worker,
Good wages,
What am I?
A: A doctor.

Sian Hammett (10)
Perrywood Primary & Nursery School, Worcester

Big Cat

Strong legs
Fierce roar
Fast runner
Meat eater
Sneak attacker
Pointy ears
Can swim
Big cat.

Travis Wiggins (10)
Perrywood Primary & Nursery School, Worcester

Hairdresser

Style specialist
Hair snipper
Shampoo setter
Good brusher
Shop owner
Colour organiser
Holiday talker
Designs hair.

Niamh Hammett (10)
Perrywood Primary & Nursery School, Worcester

Untitled

It's terrifying
Like a zombie
Blood dripping
Rotting flesh
Groans deafening
Human flesh ripper
Horrible, stupid
So disgusting.

Lewis Mitchell Hartley (10)
Perrywood Primary & Nursery School, Worcester

BMX Rider

Smooth rider,
Great staller,
Bar grinder,
High jumper,
Back flipper,
Tail whipper,
What am I?

Todd Edgington (10)
Perrywood Primary & Nursery School, Worcester

James Bond

Pistol holder
Ladies man
Window crasher
Movie actor
Trouble maker
Gadget getter.
A: James Bond.

Joshua Heywood (10)
Perrywood Primary & Nursery School, Worcester

Ninja - Haiku

Darkness arising,
Near the China coast is he,
Swift as swift can be.

Laurence Canoy (10)
Perrywood Primary & Nursery School, Worcester

Flying Football Pitch

Fans are flying in the air,
Whilst they are sitting on a plastic chair.

As the player kicks the ball,
The goalkeeper has a fall.

The football ground floats around,
It is really far off the ground.

When the ball hits the net,
Everyone knows I have won my bet.

The grass is very lush and green,
So it's very easy to be seen.

All of the fans are very vivid,
They are also all extremely livid.

The name of the ground is called Old Cloud
And the owner is very proud.

The flying football is hard to catch,
Especially with the rain coming down there is not a dry patch.

The players' tunnel here is really cool,
Because it's the size of a full-sized swimming pool.

Soaring, sweaty players curve through the air,
Mainly because there is not much space to share.

As the men fly through the air,
The wind goes through their smelly hair.

Not many people know this ground,
Even though it is the coolest place around.

The mist sometimes creeps upon this place,
And you cannot see the football player's face.

The floodlights shine upon the ground,
As if it is a big grass mound.

Clouds below us like cotton candy,
Which is sometimes quite handy.

Tom Daykin (10)
St Andrew's CE Primary School, Stafford

Giant Jelly

This giant jelly is sat on a hill,
Let me show you around, I'm Bill.

The trees are giants, looking down,
When you see it there is never a frown.

Let's get exciting, enough of the boring,
When you go inside you will feel like you are soaring.

Travel through a thick layer of jello,
You feel frozen in the layer, inside you feel mellow.

As you enter, all around is blue,
This amazing place is totally new!

Everything is jello,
To the side, up-top and below.

There are statues of ladies and men,
In this gigantic den.

Munch and gobble,
As you wobble.

Jelly is stolen by food businessmen.
What a crime, someone should sue them.

You can eat everything,
Living so big makes me want to sing.

Noise is bursting through the door,
Can there be more?

A super bounce area,
This can't get cooler.

Unfortunately, a day has to end,
Tomorrow, I wonder what's round the bend!

Finley Joseph Morris (10)
St Andrew's CE Primary School, Stafford

Engulf, Transform

Today's the day we all die
The sun will engulf us in the sky
A nuclear explosion
Brought havoc from the ocean.

Millenniums after Od was created
And invented two lions and they mated
Humans soon came
But they had a mane.

This world was luminous
Although the lights were curious
This place was transformed
Though people still mourned.

Funnel leaves on
Pink trees
Flat vines
Brilliant wines.

The rainbow of plants
But one was still in a trance
Crazy people all around
And some don't even make a sound.

In the forest like New York
Everyone still ate pork
Wine bottles don't have corks
But they still used knifes and forks.

This is from the land of Od
Can you see Od as brilliant as I can?

Gisela Ashley (10)
St Andrew's CE Primary School, Stafford

Woodland Narrative Poem

He limped to his Avatar bed
He whizzed to another form of body
He ran to the helicopter
He leaped off into the dense foliage
He sped to a monster, it retreated cautiously
He looked behind
Next thing he knew
He was under a tree, opening fire with his heavy machine gun!
He was under attack
He was fighting for his life
On an eerie, dangerous, natural planet
He was in the sight of a lethal bow and arrow
She didn't fire though,
A magical firefly sat on the tip of her arrow.
He swiftly created a torch of fire,
He killed all the creatures higher and higher
He got hungry and ate his victims.
He looked around for a place to stay
He ended up in some hay!
In the morning he woke in flash
He found a lethal bird called Nitriklo
He leaped on Nitriklo
He rode him through the woods,
Dodging tree after tree -
Plant after plant
They glided up in the air
Dodging mountains everywhere
They flew and flew for evermore!

Jacob Ratcliffe (10)
St Andrew's CE Primary School, Stafford

Another Day In Paradise

Mark went down to the well
And said an enchanting magic spell.
He closed his bright opal eyes
And hopped on the spot no more than three times.

Then suddenly he was transported to a land far, far away,
He knew from experience it was going to be an exciting day.
A cascading crystal waterfall floods into a lake of mystery,
No one knows about this place and it has no history.

A rainbow of green paints the ground not the sky
And mythical creatures fly by to say hi.
Lush grass comes up to your knee
And green vines are strangling a tree.

A neon disco is taking place,
Even some animals have a glow-up face!
Flowers and plants illuminate,
Night-time lovers, these wonders they do hate.

An island floats like cloud,
Rising up they make no sound.
It's as if you have landed in a dream,
And you listen to the babbling stream.

Even is you have been before,
To see everything you would have to book a tour.
Every step brings something new,
Come on,
Paradise is waiting for you.

Megan Washburn (10)
St Andrew's CE Primary School, Stafford

The Mysterious Monster Train

Out of the window, what do I see?
The plants turning to light,
The nocturnal animals trying to flee.

In my cabin, what do I hear?
The brakes squealing below me,
Should I fear?

In the hallway, what do I taste?
The sweets from the trolley,
The old woman at the handles trying to sell.

In the train's restaurant, what do I feel?
The soft velvet on my bottom,
And I hear the customers trying to get a better deal.

In the cockpit, what do I taste?
The fumes flooding through the window, helping the train to fly,
The forest below is like a blanket of leaves, we mustn't haste.

On the ground it looks so beautiful,
A rainbow of green with curls of light breaking through,
The vines are strangling the trees I don't dare pull.

As I walk with the group,
The plants are like electric giants,
The vines are like hoops.

The journey has finished,
It's time to go home,
I will never forget this experience.

Natasha Yewdell (10)
St Andrew's CE Primary School, Stafford

Once Upon A Magical Land

Some people say this land is scary
They step inside and feel very wary,

This place holds a lot of history
A field full of war, pain and mystery,

People thought and taught on this ground
I wonder what they ever found,

The twisted vines lift from the ground
And change from the colour of blue
To the colour of me and you.

The trees and vines make a canopy of green
But they definitely aren't mean!

The flowers are full of life
And the rocks as sharp as a knife.

There used to be a rock that lay upon this ground,
I don't think it was ever found.

It made the flowers hold powers
And made the trees be able to beg on their knees.

It made the grass dance and prance
It made the mud take a chance.

This land has been through many things in its life
But is now normal and to some scary
Which makes them very wary.

Zoe Wright (11)
St Andrew's CE Primary School, Stafford

The Unknown World

Have you ever heard of the unknown world?
The world that has never been found.
With gnomes and fairies and even flying pigs!

As you walk down the winding road,
Houses are made from mushrooms covered in red spots like blood.
Giants walking through the villages, *thud, thud, thud*!
They walk through the jungle and open a curtain of light,
Brushing the trees out of their way.

Look up to the sky in the mist,
Umbrellas to shade your fist.
Floating above the deserted islands.
If you walk down the stream you will see a powerful waterfall.

If you follow the muddy track
Your imagination will burst into life
Flying sand dunes you will see,
With trees so high as the sea.

If you go down below
Your senses will start to glow
Snakes whispering with their hiss
Monkeys squawking to each other!

This world may some day be discovered
But for now
This world isn't a dream - this is the unknown world.

Sophie Thomas (10)
St Andrew's CE Primary School, Stafford

Pandora's World

As he jumped on the mysterious floating mountain
He slipped off
And fell down onto the colourful wildness,
Down on the colourful wildness
He heard a strange noise
What's that? he thought,
What is that?
A giant black dog came out of nowhere wanting fresh meat,
He ran for his life as quick as a knife
He dived in a hole, in a rotting trunk,
He saw the black dog rush by with a very big trunk
Out he crept with his machine gun,
He ran like a bullet from a gun
The monster turned and charged
Faster and faster it charged,
He got out of the way just in time as the dog lunged,
He crashed and died,
He was the last of his kind.

Callum Coates (11)
St Andrew's CE Primary School, Stafford

My Magical Kingdom

Long, long ago people would say,
This place is strange and no one would stay.
Who would live here? Who could it be?
Maybe a mouse or maybe a bear.
Come with me, let's search around,
Up to the sky, then down to the ground.
Magical leaves dance around me,
I feel like a giant as tall as a tree.
A river like a million rainbows,
It's vivid and colourful and also flows.
It's full of ancient history,
And underneath the ground lies mystery!
Hope you visit my land again
Come anytime I don't mind when!

Isabelle Clews (10)
St Andrew's CE Primary School, Stafford

The Animal's World

Down in the jungle where the monkeys fly,
They swing and swing all day and night
The parrots are funny and they give you a fright.

The towering trees grow into the open air,
The giraffes running into their closed lair
All the animals shout, 'It's so not fair.'

All the animals running away
And sometimes they come out to play,
The glistening waterfall tumbling down.

Clambering the trees the monkeys do all day,
There is always time to play.
They want to play day or night, they always deserve a fright.

The mystery river flows, out of a rock it has no source
Visitors are heading off course
Nobody knows about the land but will it stay that way . . .?

Lucy Greenall (10)
St Andrew's CE Primary School, Stafford

Electricity

We should not leave lights on,
Or the lights will run out of power.
Same with a laptop,
If you leave your laptop on for a long time,
Your battery will run out.
With a television if you are watching
It for a long time the television will be hot.
If you leave it on and you are not watching it,
Then you will burn a hole in your pocket.
So please save electricity by switching off every socket.
We need to save electricity!

Nikita Kohli (10)
St Margaret's CE Junior School, Whitnash

Trust

Good not bad
Happy not sad
We'll be helped when we
Trust in our God.

Strong not weak
Courageous not meek
We'll be helped when we
Trust in our God.

Not selfish but sharing
Not unkind but caring
We'll be helped when we
Trust in our God.

Enemy or friend
Borrow or lend
We'll be helped when we
Trust in our God.

Laughter not tears
Dreams not fears
We'll be helped when we
Trust in our God.

No hatred just love
Be free like a dove
All is ours when
We trust in our God.

Taiya Cooper (7)
St Margaret's CE Junior School, Whitnash

Little Creature

Little creature
Nibble eater
Crawler sneaker
Scrabbling paws
Whippy tail
Midnight eyes
Snivelling nose.
A: A gerbil.

Clara Soto (9)
St Thomas More Catholic School, Kettering

I Am Angry About My Homework

I am angry about my homework
Like the trees are angry about squirrels
Like the moon is infuriated by the sun
Like the wind is furious about the calm
Like dark is enraged by light
Like a teacher is livid about bad work
I am angry about my homework.

I am angry about my homework
Like a window is angry about rain
Like ice is infuriated by warmth
Like leaves are furious about autumn
Like summer is enraged by winter
Like spring is livid about autumn
I am angry about my homework.

I am angry about my homework
Like the rain is angry with the sun
Like the sun is infuriated by the clouds
Like lightning is furious with thunder
Like electricity is enraged by thunderstorms
Like the sea is livid about thunderstorms
I am angry about my homework.

I am angry about my homework
Like trees are angry about paper
Like glaciers are infuriated by the sun
Like a cloud is furious about rain
Like black holes are enraged by living things
Like lakes are livid about streams
I am angry about my homework.

I am angry about my homework
Like land is angry about sea
Like girls are furious about boys
Like liquids are enraged by solids
Like sound is livid about silence
I am angry about my homework.

Erin Walsh (9)
St Thomas More Catholic School, Kettering

I Am Angry About . . .

I am angry about politics
Like a child is infuriated when she doesn't get her own way
Like a lion is livid when she is locked up
Like a detective is wrathful when she can't solve a case
Like the moon is furious of the sun
Like a lake is irate about a storm
I am angry about politics.

I am angry about global warming
Like a team is livid when the other team cheat
Like a desert is incensed when it rains
Like Hitler is irate about losing the war
Like a class is furious about being kept in
Like a horse is infuriated when she has a stone in her shoe
I am angry about global warming.

I am angry about gossip
Like a minnow is livid about being put on the street
Like a good friend is livid when people run away from her
Like a fox is infuriated when she doesn't get her tea
Like the Conservatives are irritated about losing the election
Like a frog is wrathful about being dissected
I am angry about gossip.

I am angry about elections
Like a spider is livid when she is squashed
Like a baby is wrathful when she doesn't get her bottle
Like a basketball is bad-tempered when it is bounced
Like an apple is infuriated when it is picked
Like a guitar is incensed about being strummed
I am angry about elections.

Lucy Bishop (10)
St Thomas More Catholic School, Kettering

Pandas

P rancing around eating bamboo
A nimals laugh as it tries to get up
N ot thinking about what it is sleeping on
D ancing around in mud
A nd then it goes to sleep and does it all again.

Jordan Elliot (9)
St Thomas More Catholic School, Kettering

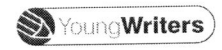

I Am Angry

I am angry about politics
Like a baby is cross when it doesn't get milk
Like a boy is livid when he doesn't score a goal
Like a pencil is irritated by an eraser
Like a storm is infuriated by the wind
Like a bee is enraged by a wasp
I am angry about politics.

I am angry at wasps
Like a door is infuriated by a lock
Like a ball is livid by a foot
Like a bull is annoyed by a child
Like a smile is incensed by crying
Like a piece of paper is bad-tempered by a laminator
I am angry at wasps.

I am angry about keys
Like a window is annoyed by lightning
Like a bulb is infuriated by a power cut
Like a car is incensed by an MOT
Like a teacher is furious at a pupil
Like a laminator is livid by a piece of paper
I am angry about keys.

I am angry about war
Like a best friend is annoyed when their friend runs away
Like an alien is irritated by a human
Like a laptop is cross at a slow typist
Like hair is livid by a brush
Like a string is bad-tempered by a needle
I am angry about war.

Alice Ball (10)
St Thomas More Catholic School, Kettering

I Am Angry . . .

I am angry about my brother
Like grass is cross with the wind
Like the trees are furious of snow
Like trees are livid at axes
Like hair is annoyed by hairclips
Like tops are irritated by jumpers
I am angry about my brother.

I am angry about my brother
Like rain is exasperated with heat
Like a pen is infuriated by a ruler
Like feet are furious at socks
Like windows are irritated by curtains
Like carpets rage at rugs
I am angry about my brother.

I am angry about my brother
Like mice are livid by traps
Like doors are annoyed by sanders
Like books are exasperated by bookmarks
Like tables rage at tablecloths
Like beds are cross at pillows
I am angry about my brother.

Leah Meghen (9)
St Thomas More Catholic School, Kettering

Like A Forest Is Anxious Of The Wind

Like a forest is anxious of the wind
Like grass is frightened of a lawn mower
Like a tambourine is terrified of a hand
Like a drum is worried of a drumstick
Like a tree is fearful of a squirrel.

Like an insect is scared of rain
Like fish are terrified of a bear
Like a cat is worried of a dog
Like a deer is frightened of a gun
Like a book is afraid of getting ripped
Like an insect is scared of rain.

Joe Massaro (9)
St Thomas More Catholic School, Kettering

I Am Happy . . .

I am happy because of football
Like a pig is joyful about mud
Like flowers are glad when it rains
Like a rabbit is ecstatic for food
Like grass is merry to grow
Like a cat is cheerful when it plays with string
I am happy because of football.

I am joyful because of FIFA 11
Like a bird is ecstatic for warmth
Like a crocodile is connected to meat
Like I am merry for half-term
Like a crow is happy to annoy people
Like a tree is pleased to grow
I am joyful because of FIFA 11.

I am happy for food
Like a panda is merry for bamboo
Like a fish is happy for water
Like we are ecstatic for the beach
Like a dog is delighted for bones
Like a workman is cheerful for a break
I am happy for food.

Aodán Farrell (9)
St Thomas More Catholic School, Kettering

Sticky Dragon

Scaly body
Slippery tongue
Changing colour
Minute by minute
Alive tongue
Creepy eyes
Insect eater
Horny head
Swaying tail
Mating frenzy.
A: Chameleon.

Myles Fletcher (9)
St Thomas More Catholic School, Kettering

I Am Happy . . .

I am happy about achieving my red belt
Like a flower is joyful about rain
Like fish are merry about the sea
Like a turtle is grateful about a beach
Like a worm is ecstatic about earth
I am happy about achieving my red belt.

I am happy today
Like a bird is delighted with spring
Like plants are joyful about sunshine
Like a seal is pleased by fish
Like a mouse is cheerful about cheese
I am happy today.

I am happy about rain
Like a tree is happy to grow
Like a bird is ecstatic to fly
Like a star is joyful when admired
Like the sun is glad to shine
I am happy about rain.

Edward Tolentino (9)
St Thomas More Catholic School, Kettering

I Am Happy Today

I am happy today
Like a knife is cheerful to be cut with
Like a hamster is jolly for his wheel
Like the crops are glad to be grown
Like the birds are merry to sing
Like the trees are pleased to be grown
I am happy today.

I am happy today
Like a spider is overjoyed for his web
Like the caterpillars are lively for their leaves
Like the flowers are lucky for water
Like a hare is ecstatic to run
Like a ship is happy to sail
I am happy today.

Anna Tew (9)
St Thomas More Catholic School, Kettering

That Spooky Thing

Clash! Smack! Bang!
The bin is raided again.
The next time I see that thing,
It's dead!
Oh, stop over exaggerating George.
(The next night)
The sound of paws tapping,
The sound of paws tapping.
Go out and have a look George,
What!
Chomp!
George are you there?
'Argh!'
A: Wolf.

Matthew Druery (9)
St Thomas More Catholic School, Kettering

I Am Scared Of . . .

I am scared of ghosts
Like a spider is scared of a foot
Like a whale is scared of a shark
Like a butterfly is scared of a net
I am scared of ghosts.

I am scared of ghosts
Like a piece of paper is scared of a pencil
Like a chair is scared of a person
Like a mouse is scared of a trap
I am scared of ghosts.

Rieno Tartaglia (9)
St Thomas More Catholic School, Kettering

Big Eyes

Big eyes
Small feet
Fluffy fur
Long tail
Whiskery nose
Pointy ears
Sharp teeth
Sneaky walk
Fast run
Good hunter.

Leilia White (9)
St Thomas More Catholic School, Kettering

Helpful Bird

Wakes people
Early bird
Loud vocal chords
Seed snatcher
Ground pecker
Large chicken
Beak lifting
Small sleeper
A: A cockerel.

James Wiles (9)
St Thomas More Catholic School, Kettering

Sticky Feet

Horny head
Scaly body
Sticky feet
Damager
Slippery tongue
Shredder body
World-wide eyes
A danger to flies.
A: Chameleon.

Luke Pallett (9)
St Thomas More Catholic School, Kettering

Night Watcher

Night watcher
Mouse eater
Bold eyes
Keen beak
Cutting talons
Feather animal
Round body
Barn animal.
A: *A barn owl.*

George Sansone (9)
St Thomas More Catholic School, Kettering

Slow Walker

Slow walker
On land
Or sea
Always green
Hates bumblebees
Likes naps
Eats skin
Lives long.
A: *Turtle.*

Daniel Hakobyan Pereira (9)
St Thomas More Catholic School, Kettering

As Black As Midnight

As black as midnight
Fast as lightning
Shy but mysterious
Playful and adorable
Suspicious eyes
Constant curiosity
Silky fur
Milk drinker.
A: *A cat.*

Nicole Pedro (9)
St Thomas More Catholic School, Kettering

Midnight Howler

Beady eyes
Gleaming moon
Scrabbling paws
Rough coat
Snarling jaws
Wild scavengers
Human killers
Midnight howler.
A: A wolf.

Emilia Berardi-Ross (9)
St Thomas More Catholic School, Kettering

Tremendous Weight

Tremendous weight
Water mate
Protective mum
Big fat tum
Food vacuum
Colossal nose
Pig's tail
Sometimes smart.
A: Hippo.

Isabella Novaga (9)
St Thomas More Catholic School, Kettering

River Fighter

Spiky teeth
Bold eyes
Crinkly body
Big blubber
Killer of many
River fighter
Sea looker
Nerdy smart.
A: A hippo.

Eva Grace Pointer (9)
St Thomas More Catholic School, Kettering

Sea Creature

Barbaric jaws
Swishing tail
Gleaming eyes
Frantic breather
Mystical fin
Dolphin eater
Sea creature
Furious swimmer.
A: A shark.

Carys Smith (10)
St Thomas More Catholic School, Kettering

Rabbit

Big eyes
Soft fur
Loves to hop
Short tail
Long ears
Pink nose
Wild and pets
Long whiskers.

Brooke Willis (9)
St Thomas More Catholic School, Kettering

He Likes Green Grass

He likes green grass
Woolly, yes he is
The place he loves
Is the field so green
With his perfect woolly coat.
A: A sheep.

Harrison Fawcett (10)
St Thomas More Catholic School, Kettering

Shark

Keen teeth
Fish eater
Big mouth
Black darter
Startling eyes
Fast swimmer.

Courtney Rusike (9)
St Thomas More Catholic School, Kettering

Twisty Tale

Greedy eater
Fat belly
Pink fur
Pointy ears
Twisty tale
Smiley face.

Charley Burke (10)
St Thomas More Catholic School, Kettering

Pinocchio

I dream of the day
When in some magic way
I'll not be a toy
But a real living boy.
It's hard to be good
I'm made out of wood.
I can't jump or talk
And need strings to walk
But one magical day
The fairy godmother would say,
'A wish to you
Make Pinocchio new
A real living
Boy!'

J R (10)
Simon De Senlis Primary School, Northampton

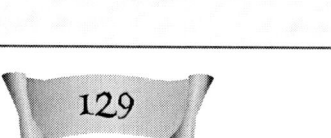

The Three Little Pigs

There was Percy, Pippa and Pinky - the three pigs
Pippa's house was made of twigs
Percy's was made out of lots of hay
Although he had lots to pay
Pinky's house was made of bricks
Everyone took their pick.

One day a grey hairy wolf came along
He went up the hill and sang a song
Wolfy knocked on Pippa's door
Pippa felt, 'Oh no I'm poor.'

Pippa went, opened the door and stood scared
There was a giant wolf outside and very grey-haired
Pippa screamed, 'You're very grey and hairy
So out there you will stay!'

Wolfy blew down Pippa's house
And let out a horrible mouse
Wolfy went to Percy's door
Percy felt, 'I'm poor.'

Percy didn't answer
Wolfy thought he was a dancer
Wolfy blew down Percy's house
And once again let out a mouse.

Wolfy walked on to Pinky's door
He didn't answer because he felt too poor
Wolfy could not blow down Pinky's house
He just let out another mouse.

The other pigs went to Pinky's door
Pinky let them in even though they were poor
They all lived together happily ever after
The wolf was gone and they had so much laughter.

Amy Bean (9)
Simon De Senlis Primary School, Northampton

Red Riding Hood

Once there was a little girl
Called Red Riding Hood.
She lived with her Mum,
Also she was very good.

One day she said, 'Take this pie,
To your lovely gran.'
She had a little sigh
And then she ran.

She went on,
Until she saw a little house.
'That is my gran's,'
She said, as quiet as a mouse.

Before Red Riding Hood set her feet in to the door,
A big bad wolf caught sight of her.
The big bad wolf already had lunch but he always wanted more.
The wolf had a good idea to pretend to be Gran,

So he did
And then chucked the real gran in the bin.
When he was tricking Red Riding Hood,
The woodcutter came in and the wolf didn't win.

They freed Gran from the bin,
They had a couple of cheers,
Then Gran said,
'Oh, thank you dears!'

Ellie Thorpe (9)
Simon De Senlis Primary School, Northampton

Minotaur

M ean and murderous, never lies
I ncredible and enormous, always carries an axe
N otorious and nasty, never spares a life
O gre and obscene, blood he likes the most
T errifying and torturous, horns can set on fire
A ngry and annoying, lives in a volcano
U nkind and unliked, furriest of them all
R aging and roaring, he's waiting to charge.

Callum Perrin (10)
Simon De Senlis Primary School, Northampton

The Three Little Pigs

There were three little pigs,
One whose house was made of twigs,
The pigs all took their pick,
And a wise pig chose bricks.

Then a bad wolf came there,
And blew mad as a bear,
He frightened the whole place,
Not just with his mad face.

A brave pig came along,
And played some good pig pong,
He most happily won,
And then the wolf was done.

One of the pigs was there,
And ran fast as a hare,
'Yes, yes, yes,' he said,
And he jumped up and fled.

The wolf blew a pig's house down,
And the pig looked like a clown,
The pig with the bricked house,
Scared the wolf like a mouse.

For he was burnt with fire,
Forever he was a liar!

Ayo Arowolo (9)
Simon De Senlis Primary School, Northampton

Tutankhamen

Tutankhamen was as powerful as can be.
He ruled to precisely 1327BC.
He made a great pyramid for when he was dead.
A great ruler of Egypt lay silently in his bed.
He went to the afterlife to see all the dead.
The thought of a new king filled the Egyptians with dread.
The Pharaoh ruled Egypt, he had lots of gold.
When he was buried he felt alone and cold.
He waited 5,000 years for his story to be told.
Then 5,000 years later an archaeologist cracked his code.

Jamie Hayday (9)
Simon De Senlis Primary School, Northampton

The Three Little Pigs

'Mummy Pig, Mummy Pig, I am getting too old,
Your house is about to be sold.
I need to move in the grove,
I am going to pack my bags, can you help me?

Can I have some sticks to build my house?'
'Yeah sure, but get me a mouse.'
The pig got the mouse and the mum got the sticks,
'Can my brother have some bricks?'

They built their houses nice and strong,
Then the other came along.
Mummy Pig gave him some straw and a rotten old door,
'Can you help me build my house?' 'Sure.'

They built his house in a nickey,
Nice and strong but not too tricky.
Along came the wolf and blew it down,
And they ran into his brother's house.

The sticks house was made nice and strong,
The wolf came along and blew it down.
The pigs ran into the brick house,
Along came the wolf, he could not blow it down.
He was scared of a tiny little mouse!
The wolf ran away for 20 odd days.

Matthew Duffy (10)
Simon De Senlis Primary School, Northampton

Unicorns And Pegasus

Unicorns are pale with shrines of cheer
So believe your magic with a merry smile
But have no moods
Sing a song to keep your precious smile.
Pegasus is black like a devil
So don't be greedy or even murder
Your spirit will go to Heaven
So you will see a unicorn
However end up in Hell
A Pegasus will be there!

Sam Nurse (10)
Simon De Senlis Primary School, Northampton

Black Beauty

When Black Beauty was born,
There were very merry faces.
But Black Beauty didn't care
She just liked going at different paces.

One day in the barn, a man was smoking,
A boy told him to stop.
But he thought he was joking,
When the horses went to bed,
A fire lit and spread.

Black Beauty was out first, but Ginger didn't come
He'd already lost his mother
He couldn't lose his lover.
Black Beauty grew up a slave
Ginger too, but all that time they learnt to be brave.

One day while driving a carriage,
Ginger's body came past.
Black Beauty hung his head in sadness
But inside was madness.

After Ginger's death
There wasn't a lot left
For Black Beauty but he had a life
And Ginger was in his heart.

Kate Skinner (9)
Simon De Senlis Primary School, Northampton

Robin Hood

Robin Hood is a joy,
He likes fighting with his boys.
Robin, Robin, I need help!
I bit myself and I yelped.
Robin, Robin, save my boy,
And I'll save his big toys.
Robin Hood is his name.
But he doesn't play a game.
Robin Hood came to Nottingham
And he was playing with his horse and he was trotting him.

Chloe Higgins-White (9)
Simon De Senlis Primary School, Northampton

Once Upon a Rhyme – Poets From The Midlands

Hansel And Gretel

Once in a lonely, lonely wood,
Two little children stood.
Because of their stepmother's groans,
They left a trail of stones.

By following the trail of stone,
They managed to get home.
All they were given was some bread,
When their stepmother said.

They both disappeared from their house,
As quiet as a mouse.
They found a big house made of sweets,
It had marzipan sheets.

They met an evil, evil witch,
The witch was very rich.
She wanted to eat them for her tea,
But they found her key.

They escaped together that night,
But they put up a fight.
Slamming the oven on her head,
They grabbed some coins and fled.

Evie Stanton (9)
Simon De Senlis Primary School, Northampton

Bang! There's Fireworks

Bang! There's fireworks
Up in the sky, shimmering bright,
What a lovely sight.
There in the sky, I hear not one sigh,
I love fireworks at night,
They are always brightening up my life.

Wow, they're different shapes.
What do they make?
I love them all and many people they wake.
I love fireworks,
They always shine so bright,
The fireworks are always working as a light.

Tia Binks (10)
Simon De Senlis Primary School, Northampton

Ocean

As I stand on the beach
And watch the sea,
The lonely seagulls
Talk to me.

As I draw my attention
From the air,
The sea starts tossing
Everywhere.

A storm starts brewing,
The air gets cold,
The tide comes in,
The waves are bold.

As the tide
Comes ever nearer,
One vital sign
Is ever clearer.

I dive into the sea
And as it starts to hail,
I swim ever deeper
With a flick of my tail.

Jasmin Cox (10)
Simon De Senlis Primary School, Northampton

Medusa

What did Medusa do to her hair?
Whoever looks at her turns to stone.
How does Medusa use her powers?
Why does Medusa turn people into grey stone?
She looks weird, snakes in her hair.
She turns people to stone to get revenge.
How did she get snakes in her hair?
Was she like that when she was born?
She hated snakes in her hair.
She hated everyone.
Medusa, Medusa she's got the maddest hair.
Medusa's arch enemy is Perseus.

Lewis Bradley (9)
Simon De Senlis Primary School, Northampton

The Three Little Pigs

There once were three little pigs
And they were getting too big
So they said bye to their mum
And sucked their thumbs as they left.

The first pig was a bit dim because he made his house of straw
And then came a wolf with the power of a bull
And the pig went out of the window.

The wolf said, 'Little Pig, Little Pig, let me in.'
The pig replied, 'Not on the hair of my chinny, chin, chin'
The wolf said, 'Then I'll huff and I'll puff and I'll blow your house down.'

He blew it down and ate the pig and the wolf faced the other house not made of straw, made of sticks,
The wolf came along and said, 'Little Pig, Little Pig, let me in.'
He said, 'Not by the hair of my chinny, chin, chin.
The wolf said, 'Then I'll huff and I'll puff and blow your house down.'

The wolf came to another pig,
But he didn't build his house of straw or sticks,
He made it from bricks.
The wolf took a breath as hard as he could,
It didn't fall, it stood!

Ash Tailor (8)
Simon De Senlis Primary School, Northampton

The Wavy Sea

The sea is blue, wavy too.
Spraying water at you.
Splashing on the rocks
Making a huge *crash!*
Making the seaweed stay on the rocks.
Wind blowing in your face,
When you step on the sand,
Makes us cold as can be.
Whales with their calf teaching how to swim,
Divers swimming, finding small,
Sea horses, dolphins,
Jumping up and down.

Jade Walter (10)
Simon De Senlis Primary School, Northampton

Odysseus And The Cyclops

Odysseus had to find the golden fleece.
So then there would be more world peace.
He got in his ship made of wood.
In the centre the mast stood.
At the end of the journey he saw.
A cave full of blood and gore.
A hideous sight!
A fist of dynamite!
A Cyclops as big as a house!
Who was eating a giant mouse!
Odysseus looked . . .
He was going to get cooked . . .
He swiped its head clean off its shoulders!
It came down like a ton of boulders!
He poked its head.
It was dead.
The golden fleece was back in its home
The Cyclops was buried in an underground dome.

Jordan Harrison (9)
Simon De Senlis Primary School, Northampton

Deep Blue Sea

Down in the ocean where the sea animals live.
Electric eels shock you day and night, the pain comes.
Every day fish swim in the cold sea.
People relax by the sea.

Butterflies fly over the sea.
Little dolphins jumping through the sea.
Under the sea the sand is soft and wet.
Eagles dive down at the sea for fish.

Sand is soft and falls through your hands.
Every day crabs go *click, click*.
As you walk across the beach your feet sink
Into the sand.

Kelson Gibbons (10)
Simon De Senlis Primary School, Northampton

Crash! Goes The Sea

Crash! goes the sea,
Blue as can be.
Filling all the rock pools,
Crash! goes the sea.

Bang! goes the sea,
Climbing up the cliffs.
Eating all the beach,
Bang! goes the sea.

Flash! There's a storm,
Upsetting the sea.
Here comes the white horses,
Flash! There's a storm.

Crash! goes the sea,
Blue as can be.
Filling all the rock pools,
Crash! goes the sea.

Tia Binks (10)
Simon De Senlis Primary School, Northampton

Polluted Sea

The sea swirls slowly
The sea is clean
While the coconut trees are growing
The salt goes to the sea.

The factories are rumbling
The power sources are dirty
They put hot water to the sea
The fish die from hot water.

The eco humans have came to save us
They block the water to a river
The fish are now living
The trees live once again!

David Obreja (10)
Simon De Senlis Primary School, Northampton

The Three Little Pigs

There were three little pigs,
One had a house made of twigs.
If you want to call them sticks,
One had a house made of bricks.

I remember there was one more,
He made a house out of straw.
But a wolf came down to spy,
He only spied with one eye.

The wolf blew the straw house down,
The poor pig felt like a clown.
The house of sticks went down quick,
He tried to fight with his stick.

For the house made of bricks,
That clever pig had some tricks.
But when the wolf came to spy,
He was turned into a pie!

Oliver Fosbury (9)
Simon De Senlis Primary School, Northampton

The Three Little Pigs

The three little pigs liked to splash in mud,
But it got dirty all the time.
They went upstairs and washed their butts
After they drank some wine.

Then they got ready for the park,
But then it got very foggy,
They stopped and got very daft,
Then they got soggy.

One day a pig built a house with straw,
But then it started to rain,
He really liked to get all wet,
But then he went very insane.

Len Mwaura (9)
Simon De Senlis Primary School, Northampton

Pinocchio - The Dream

I dream far away of the day
We will be living in a magic way
I will not be a toy
I will be a real living boy.

It is so hard to be good
When I'm made out of wood
With my nose so long
I cannot be strong.

I'll always be weak
But never peak
I might sigh
But I will never die.

I will always be clever
But never watch the weather
I will always have a long nose
But this I never chose.

Abbie Reboul (9)
Simon De Senlis Primary School, Northampton

Round And Round

Swirling round and round
Will I every stop?
This life is making me dizzy
Oh will I ever stop?

I want to leave this life
Please help me
The everlasting movement
Oh please help me.

I crash against the mainland
Free I am once more
My fellow waves are edging me away
From the thing I love the most.

Gabriella Teriaca (10)
Simon De Senlis Primary School, Northampton

Scuba-Diving

On the beach it has
Loads of annoying leaches
That look like peaches
On the beach.

Under the sea, it's bright
And makes me feel light
Like a termite
At night.

Under the rocks
There are flocks of
Little heart-shaped rocks
Under the rocks in the sea.

Ryan Wright (10)
Simon De Senlis Primary School, Northampton

Neptune's Sea

Neptune is the god of the angry sea
But he loves everything he sees.
He's got 50,000 hardworking servants
And great they must be.

He loves making curly waves
And very tall tides
But whoever is bad
They must get *fried!*

Wherever he goes he must have back-up
Even 250 feet down, he must not die
If King Neptune dies or gets hurt
There will never ever be any sea *again!*

William Jack Rainbow
Simon De Senlis Primary School, Northampton

The Shimmering Sunset

As I stand upon the bright blue ocean
I hear the seagulls sing
They flutter over me
As I eagerly watch the sea.

They make a squawking sound
As I hear the ocean rumbling
I know the tide is coming
Out of the bright blue sea.

The sand is yellow
And makes me feel happy
As I play and throw the sand around
I feel like it wants to play with me.

Rhumer Kay (11)
Simon De Senlis Primary School, Northampton

Peter pan

Mama says she wants us to stay,
But I want to go on holiday.
So I asked my brothers to hurry up
Then out the window we flew.

The Lost Boys shot Wendy in the heart,
And Tink said that was smart.
While that happened John and Michael got caught.

Peter Pan went to kill Captain Hook,
But Captain Hook didn't look.
He fell into the crocodile's mouth,
Off home we flew!

Megan Schofield (9)
Simon De Senlis Primary School, Northampton

A Day In The Sea

As I walk up to the sea,
I smell a storm coming near me.

I set my umbrella right in the ground
And see the waves going round and round.

I hear the seagulls talking to me,
I wonder what they're saying.

I taste the water in my mouth,
Hoping I can go in it now!

When I go in the water, I feel so alive
But as I go further, the storm feels alive.

Shivani Sehmi
Simon De Senlis Primary School, Northampton

This Is The Place I Like To Be

As I put my feet in the sea
I see the pink shells underneath me.

As I see the orange crabs crawling about
The seagulls screech out loud.

I can see the shimmering sea
This is the place I like to be.

As I walk closer to the sea
The breeze is coming towards me.

I can see the shimmering sea
This is the place I like to be.

Emily Nicklin (10)
Simon De Senlis Primary School, Northampton

Medusa

Medusa needs to comb her hair for there are knots everywhere,
When she cuts her hair,
There are loads of screams everywhere.
Don't go anywhere because Medusa is coming out there.
Open your eyes, you will get a big surprise.

Bhavika Mistry (9)
Simon De Senlis Primary School, Northampton

The Ocean

As the dolphins jump in and out
Of the blue waves,
The ocean glistens gently through
The day.

As the waves crash against the grey,
Jagged rocks,
The seaweed makes a pattern on
The face of the rocks.

Little fishes finding their way to safety,
As the gloomy seas cover the golden sands.

Jasmin West (10)
Simon De Senlis Primary School, Northampton

Underwater Disco

The seaweed boogies
The crabs jive,
The fish swirl,
The starfish dive!

The whales quick step,
The swordfish tango,
The waves crash,
In time!

Not many people know,
Of the underwater disco.

Natasha Partridge (10)
Simon De Senlis Primary School, Northampton

Egyptian God Poem

Amun, the great god of creation in different forms
Ra, with the sun on his head - he does not make the storms
Nut, God of the Sky up so high
Geb, God of Earth down there he lie
With the scale Anubis weighs your bad heart
He throws it into Sobek like a dart.

Jamie Vaughan (9)
Simon De Senlis Primary School, Northampton

The Sea

As I sit on
The beach alone
I hear the sea
Talking to me.

I hear the sea
Smashing and crashing
Up against the beach.

As I get up and walk into the sea,
With a flick of my tail
I'm gone into the deep blue sea.

Nathan Cox (10)
Simon De Senlis Primary School, Northampton

The Mad Sea

The mad sea
Hurtling to the rocks
With the white horses
Coming out to catch you
As it washes you away in the deep.

The mad sea
Everyone coming to drag
You back to land
But the sea is so strong.

Olivia Dugmore (10)
Simon De Senlis Primary School, Northampton

The Minotaur

The Minotaur as big as three men.
The incredibly strong beast lurks in the maze.
His noisy roar pierces your ears.
His hooves on the ground make you freeze to the core.
He tears through flesh like knives through butter.
The anxious beast is never defeated.
The official king of the beasts.
Run away, it's the Minotaur.

Callum Kennedy (9)
Simon De Senlis Primary School, Northampton

Peter Pan And Captain Hook

Come with me to a place called Neverland
Far, far away and you will find
Captain Hook, the pirate, and his pirate men
To you find lots of magical things.

Meet the Lost Boys and see the giant waterfall
And you find the crocodile in the lake swimming around
I will fight Captain Hook when I can
While you're making tea
And in the evening we can fly around the clouds.

Jamie Collingwood (10)
Simon De Senlis Primary School, Northampton

Ocean

Sparkling ocean in the sunlight
Every single drop of the sun
Focusing on the ocean
Splish, splash, splosh
Everyone adores it
Splash, splash, splash
Now night has come
The ocean is dazzling in the moonlight
And everyone has gone home.

Hannah Chisholm (10)
Simon De Senlis Primary School, Northampton

The Ocean And The Sandy Sunset

I walk along the beach
Searching for more shells
Listening to the seagulls screech
Sitting on the shore swishing my feet round
Suddenly it's sunset and I can't hear a sound
The sea is glimmering
The sea is shimmering
Dolphins are jumping in and out
Crabs are scuttling all about.

Chloe Scott (10)
Simon De Senlis Primary School, Northampton

The Beautiful Sea

The waves crash,
As the white horses come,
The animals play,
And have lots of fun.

Splash! The waves go,
Over and over.
Quiet and tranquil
Or strong and mighty.

Poppy Jones (10)
Simon De Senlis Primary School, Northampton

Sunlight

As I look into the water
My eyes gleaming bright
Reflecting in the water
And shining so bright.

The water crashes against
The hard rocky walls
Hoping there will be more
And this is the place for me.

Ella Clarke (10)
Simon De Senlis Primary School, Northampton

Mystery Ocean

Mystery, mystery, like the sea,
Apple pie with a cup of tea,
Sitting on the sand with a bun in my hand,
That's what I see.

As I am in the fair,
I can see the waves bashing in the air,
Seagulls flying in the sky,
As I am saying goodbye.

Lewis Gilmour (11)
Simon De Senlis Primary School, Northampton

Hercules

H eroic
E nergetic
R emarkable
C urious
U nbeatable
L azy
E cstatic
S trong.

Christopher Amankonah (10)
Simon De Senlis Primary School, Northampton

The Elegant Sea

I feel the grainy sand slipping through my hands.
The deep sea, blue as ever can be.
The white horses gallop toward me.
The light seagulls talk to me.
Within the light blue sky I feel so alive.
When the sea takes over me.
I see the beautiful creatures of the sea.
The sea is like a flower blossoming among the waves.

Joshua Nkire (10)
Simon De Senlis Primary School, Northampton

Odysseus

Odysseus is the bravest man
He's fierce, he's bold and stronger than a goat
If you want to fight him you have no chance
Because he will kill you and you'll never come back
He can break a stone with just his arms
If you're near him you'd better run
Because he is coming and he's stronger than before.

Rajinder Singh Thandi (10)
Simon De Senlis Primary School, Northampton

Sea

The tide comes in
The horses gallop along the sea
With the seagulls in the sky
The sea is blue
The starfish are red
The boat that sank with the dead passengers is covered with leftover bones.

Tyler Paul Allen Maishment (10)
Simon De Senlis Primary School, Northampton

Seaside

S eagulls in the sky,
E vil waves crashing by,
A dventurous people under the sea,
S ee the surfers riding the waves,
I see the wind coming by,
D eep under the sea the creatures live,
E vil waves come by.

Olivia Wingrove (11)
Simon De Senlis Primary School, Northampton

There She Blows

Bash, crash goes the sea
I wonder what it would be
When I'm sailing out to sea
The smooth waves coming to shore
Under my feet fresh, cold water
The beautiful fish in the ocean
As the sun sets the water shines with fame and glory.

Jack Baker (10)
Simon De Senlis Primary School, Northampton

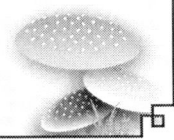

The Amazing Seaside

S parkly ocean
E very drop of you shines
A eroplanes slow down because of you
S *plash, splash, splash*
I n the daytime
D azzle the sea creatures
E ven *you!*

Husna Khawaja (10)
Simon De Senlis Primary School, Northampton

Medusa

It is so hard to do my hair
Because people scream
And they are all so mean
And say I'm unclean
That is why I turn people to stone
Because I'm left all alone
With no friends in my home.

Chloe Holder (10)
Simon De Senlis Primary School, Northampton

Untitled

As I sat by the ocean
It looked like poison
Then I sat on the beach
And saw a beak.
I looked at a boat
Then suddenly choked
I said, 'No, don't.'

Keanu Cross (10)
Simon De Senlis Primary School, Northampton

The Sea

White horses riding inwards
As the tide comes up.

Blue dolphins jumping in
And out of the sea.

Starfish stuck to the orange wet sand
In the rock pools as the sea comes in.

Bradley Luis-Hobbs (10)
Simon De Senlis Primary School, Northampton

The Evil Sea

The sea is like a pitchfork
Glowing in the dark
The rocks all shimmer and glimmer
Purple, blue and dark
It lights up your day
Young or old.

Jordan Glentworth (10)
Simon De Senlis Primary School, Northampton

Bash Goes The Sea

Bash goes the sea,
As bad as it can be,
Flash goes the camera,
Admiring the deep blue sea,
Creatures in the sea,
As creepy and crawly as you can be!

Jack Dredge (10)
Simon De Senlis Primary School, Northampton

The Three Little Pigs

P ink, poor and proud.
I ntelligent, important and interesting.
G entle, genius and generous.
S pecial, strong and skilful.

Jack Smith (10)
Simon De Senlis Primary School, Northampton

Deep In The Sea

With a flick of the tail
The dolphins are down deep
If you watch you'll see them swimming with the fishes
With an eek and a squeak the eels hiss
Tell me a storm's coming
That means I'm going!

Lucy Marsh (10)
Simon De Senlis Primary School, Northampton

The Seaside Waves

Whirling winds
Atrocious waves
Vicious white horses galloping near
Evil skies heading my way
Seagulls flying in the stormy sky.

Elizabeth Powell (11)
Simon De Senlis Primary School, Northampton

The Sea

The sea is blue.
The seagulls flew
With the boat that set sail and the gigantic whale.
When tide comes in,
There's a sight of a dolphin.

Edward Barrett (10)
Simon De Senlis Primary School, Northampton

Ocean Blue

Whistling winds
Birds circling around me
Crashing waves
Bang, pop, smash
Colourful rainbows dipping in and out of the sea.

Ciara Mulcahy (10)
Simon De Senlis Primary School, Northampton

The Dark Side Of The Sea

The sea is bad,
Crashing on the shore.
Taking everyone in.
Sinking ships killing humans,
This is why the sea is bad.

CJ Mlilo (11)
Simon De Senlis Primary School, Northampton

The Egyptian God Creator

Once there was nothing on Earth,
Just a little egg
Suddenly one day out popped a massive leg
Out came an Egyptian God called Ra
He was the God of the sky, the sun and the stars.

Bethany Lam (9)
Simon De Senlis Primary School, Northampton

The Egyptian God Creator

Once there was nothing on Earth apart from a little egg.
Suddenly one day the egg cracked and out popped a huge leg.
He was an Egyptian God called Amun
He was alone but the Egyptian's would worship him soon.

Megan Topham (9)
Simon De Senlis Primary School, Northampton

Magnificent Sea

The glistening sea rocks forward and backwards,
As children splash in and out.
Galloping towards us the sea so fast,
The white horses stop and sink in the waves.

Bethany Winter (10)
Simon De Senlis Primary School, Northampton

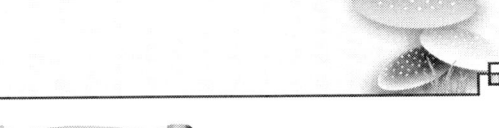

The Crystal Sky

I love the sky,
When I'm beside the sea,
Especially at night,
Because it inspires me.

Rhys Jenkins (10)
Simon De Senlis Primary School, Northampton

Lucy And Faith's Emotions

Faith was ecstatic like a buzzing bumblebee
As she walked into school to collect her award
Lucy was as delightful as a Jack-in-the-box
Her best friend was coming round to her house.

Faith was as cheerful as a tiger running through the overgrown jungle,
As she walked up the school steps
Lucy was as jealous as a ragdoll as her twin bought a brand new coat and wore it to school.

Faith was as scared as a mouse squeaking
Through a big black dark haunted house.
Lucy was as miserable as a black and stormy night
As it was her spelling test the next day.

Faith was as mischievous as a monkey swinging through the rainforest as she had copied her friend's work.

Lucy Irons (9) & Faith Burrill (10)
Stanwick School, Stanwick

Autumn

I was sitting there watching, watching the autumn slowly pass by.
I saw people dragging their feet behind them like the wind dragging a scarf behind you.
I could hear the trees rustling like when you'd shiver if a ghost went woo!
I saw the leaves dropping from the trees like red, yellow and gold confetti, at a beautiful wedding.
I saw the cut grass on the ground like a comfy bed,
So as I sat there quietly watching on a lovely autumn day
I am thanking for what we all have, for all the crops and more.

Charlotte Irons (9)
Stanwick School, Stanwick

Autumn Feelings

The dirt is as dry as the sand on a desert
The wind blows the dirt over my shoes
And makes my socks as dirty as a pig
That hasn't been washed in weeks.

The wind is as cold as ice
That has just got out the freezer
The breeze gently moves the leaves
That sit on the thick branches.

You can hear the children shout
As loudly as a newborn baby's cry
You can hear them playing with
Their friends as they kick the ball.

Isabelle Aubrey (9)
Stanwick School, Stanwick

Sitting In Autumn

As I sat in the cold autumn wind,
I felt as cold as ice,
Like I would freeze any minute.

I watched the leaves fall softly to the ground,
Some as yellow as paint,
Others as brown as wood.

As I stepped on the leaves they rustled like a plastic bag,
The whoosh that the leaves made,
Made me feel calm and relaxed and forget all my worries.

Natasha Blakemore (9)
Stanwick School, Stanwick

Cheerful

The boy was as cheerful as a jumping kangaroo.
He got a new dog and called it Sue.
He had a gleaming smile like a sparkling moon.
Then the boy put on a cheerful tune.
The boy started dancing and grabbed a red balloon.

Nathaniel Gyngell (9)
Stanwick School, Stanwick

Autumn

When the autumn arrives and darker night draw,
The golden leaves have fallen to the ground
And the benches are as cold as snow.

When leaves fall they can be all different colours
Some can be as gold as coins
And some as red as leaping fire.

When I walk to school in the early morning sunshine
I walk through a field and the freshly cut grass
Fills my head with excitement.

Emma Brown (10)
Stanwick School, Stanwick

Autumn Days!

As I walked, I could see colourful leaves
Like pieces of rainbow falling from the sky.

As I walked I could feel the air
Like a fan in my face.

As I walked, I could smell
The fresh flowers like wonderful perfume.

As I walked, I could hear
Buzzing bees like an alarm clock.

Zach Martin-Sinclair (10)
Stanwick School, Stanwick

One Autumn Day

As I sat down on a cold autumn day,
I heard the birds tweeting like Cheryl Cole,
It brought a smile to my face and a tune to my head.
As I walked down the new fresh grass
It smelt like a baby that has just been born,
It took me to a wonderful peaceful summer day with my family.
As I looked down onto the floor
I saw lots of beautiful colours of leaves
It looked like butterfly wings spread out across the floor.

Amy Delauney (9)
Stanwick School, Stanwick

Autumn

A nimals are going south for winter
U nder the tree leaves are fallen
T umbling leaves crackling like sparklers on Bonfire Night
U nderneath the leaves hedgehogs sleep
M illions of leaves falling to the ground
N oisy birds tweeting as they fly through the air.

Elise Hodge (9)
Stanwick School, Stanwick

Halloween

Chocolate, scary
Dressing up, haunted
Halloween
Trick or treat, sweets.

Joshua Dawson (9)
Stanwick School, Stanwick

Snowman - Haiku

Snowman made of ice
Like a dead man in the snow
Sun rising, oh no.

Rory Vartanian (9)
Stanwick School, Stanwick

In The Canteen

Ellie is eating
Brodie's burping
Charlie's chomping chewy chocolate
Megan's munching mouldy mushrooms.

I chomp crunchy cabbage
I slurp slushy strawberry shakes
I gobble green grapes
I like healthy food
In the canteen.

Brodie Edge (7)
Whitchurch CE Junior School, Whitchurch

Food Attack

I gobble banoffee
I munch lamb
I chew toffee
I nibble ham.

I like greens
I munch jam
I like beans
I guzzle clams.

I like lollipops
I like Cadbury's Flake
I munch lamb chops
I like tuna bake.

I like coffee
I munch lamb
I like toffee
I gobble jam.

Charles Smith (7)
Whitchurch CE Junior School, Whitchurch

In The Canteen

Megan's munching
Ellis is eating
Brodie's burping
Sam's sucking
Tilly is tasting
Charlie's crunching
Nathan's nibbling
Peter's picking
Cameron's chewing
Graham is gobbling
Chris is crushing
Sallie is swallowing
In the canteen.

Megan Stokes (7)
Whitchurch CE Junior School, Whitchurch

In The Canteen

Tiffany is tasting
Ellie's eating
Stephanie's slurping
Tilly's taking
Nathan's nibbling
Brodie's burping
Jimmy's guzzling
Scott's slushing
River's rushing
Luke's licking
Charlie's chopping
Claire is crunching
In the canteen.

Tiffany Chan (7)
Whitchurch CE Junior School, Whitchurch

In The Canteen

Scott is slobbering
Ciaran's crunching
Sally's slurping
Gayle's gobbling
Brodie is burping
Mollie's munching
Ellie is eating
Stephanie is sucking
River's tummy is rumbling
Luke's licking
Cally's crunching
Gordon is grinding
In the canteen.

Abby Rooney (7)
Whitchurch CE Junior School, Whitchurch

In The Canteen

Sam is slurping
Cameron is crunching
Brodie's burping
Tilly is tasting
Charlie is chopping
Nathan's nibbling
Scott is sipping
Peter is peeling
Ellie is eating
Megan is munching
Owen is grinning.

Cameron Jones (7)
Whitchurch CE Junior School, Whitchurch

Lovely Food

I lick lollies
I crunch clams
I nibble fries
I chew hams
I slurp milk
I gobble cake
I munch ice cream
I chomp steak
Mmm . . . lovely food.

Tilly Evanson (7)
Whitchurch CE Junior School, Whitchurch

Lovely Food

I munch apples
I crunch lamb
I guzzle grapes
I gobble jam
I suck sweets
I munch steak
I slurp milkshake
I crunch cake.

Holly Millerchip (7)
Whitchurch CE Junior School, Whitchurch

In The Canteen

Scott is slobbering
Megan's munching
Tyler is tasting
Charlie's chomping
Brodie's burping
Ellie's eating
Nelly nibbles nasty nuts
In the canteen.

James Maddocks (7)
Whitchurch CE Junior School, Whitchurch

In The Canteen

Scott is slobbering
Kinsey is crushing
Tyler is tasting
Charlie is chucking
Brodie is burping
Luke is licking
In the canteen.

Owen Kinsey (7)
Whitchurch CE Junior School, Whitchurch

Untitled

Tyler is tasting
Charlie's chomping
I munch chocolate
I guzzle pineapple cake
Ellie is eating
James like jam.

Tyler Ashley (7)
Whitchurch CE Junior School, Whitchurch

In The Canteen

I gobble noodles
I slurp milkshake
I guzzle pineapple
I munch chocolate cake.

Alex Williams (8)
Whitchurch CE Junior School, Whitchurch

Young Writers Information

We hope you have enjoyed reading this book - and that you will continue to enjoy it in the coming years.

If you like reading and writing poetry drop us a line, or give us a call, and we'll send you a free information pack.

Alternatively, if you would like to order further copies of this book or any of our other titles, then please give us a call or log onto our website at www.youngwriters.co.uk.

Young Writers Information
Remus House
Coltsfoot Drive
Peterborough
PE2 9BF
Tel: (01733) 890066
Fax: (01733) 313524

Email: info@youngwriters.co.uk

Shakespeare Quiz Answers

1. Stratford-upon-Avon 2. Romeo and Juliet 3. James I 4. 18 5. The Tempest 6. Regan, Cordelia and Goneril 7. His wife 8. Venice 9. All's Well That Ends Well, As You Like It, The Comedy of Errors, Cymbeline, Love's Labour's Lost, Measure for Measure, The Merchant of Venice, The Merry Wives of Windsor, A Midsummer Night's Dream, Much Ado About Nothing, Pericles - Prince of Tyre, The Taming of the Shrew, The Tempest, Twelfth Night, The Two Gentlemen of Verona, Troilus & Cressida, The Winter's Tale 10. Henry V 11. Claire Danes 12. Macbeth 13. Hamlet 14. Sonnet